For Love of Daniel

By

John Isaac Jones

Table of Contents

Jack and Frances 1

Visitor 9

Daniel.. 18

Exodus 27

Mildred 35

Raising Daniel 44

The Accident 52

School 56

Custody hearing 61

Jack's Transformation.............................. 73

Suzanne's Return 83

The Hearing 88

The Hand-over 101

For Love of Daniel

Jack and Frances

North Alabama, 1955

Jack Griffin woke up. He rubbed his right eye, his good one, then rolled over and glanced at the clock. It was 6:35, Monday morning. He had to be at work at eight. Through the window, he could see a gray, overcast sky and hear light rain clinking on the window panes. Jack sat up in bed, stretched his arms, and threw his feet on the floor. Moments later, he was dressed and in the kitchen. Quickly, he cleared the previous night's dishes and food scraps off the table, then wiped it clean with a damp cloth. Then he grabbed an oak water bucket sitting beside the sink and headed to the well. Every morning, once he was awake and dressed, the first thing he did was go to the well.

Outside, the rain was a light drizzle as he strode across the yard. He dropped the metal bucket into the well, then jiggled the rope until the bucket fell on its side and started to fill. Once filled, he hefted the metal bucket up and poured the water into the wooden container. Back inside, he placed the full water bucket beside the sink and began preparing two bologna and mayonnaise sandwiches. Once finished, he placed the sandwiches, along with two apples and a store-bought sweet cake, into a small black lunch pail. Then he dipped cold beef stew out of a pot into a bowl, grabbed two cold biscuits, and sat down to eat. Suddenly, remembering there was no milk, he got up.

Moments later, he was strolling across Highway 17 to the home of Miss Frances Hathaway, his neighbor who lived across the street.

"Morning, Miss Hathaway."

"Morning, Jack," she said, opening the door. "Don't look! Let me get my wig."

Jack stood in the doorway and politely looked away as she went to the corner of the living room, then, standing in front of a mirror, hastily pulled a black wig over her head. Satisfied she was presentable, she turned back at Jack.

"You know I can't face the world without my wig."

"Can I get some fresh milk?"

"I don't have a full gallon. I got maybe half a gallon."

"That will be fine."

Jack watched as she went to the refrigerator in the kitchen and returned moments later with a container of fresh milk.

"Thank you, Miss Hathaway!" he said, taking the container.

He pressed fifty cents into her hand and turned to go.

"Will you look at the light in my pantry?" Frances said. "I can't get it to come on. I've changed the bulb."

"Can it wait until this afternoon? I got to be at work in an hour."

"That will be fine."

For Love of Daniel

Moments later, jug of milk in hand, Jack was walking back across the highway to his home. As he walked, Jack struck the portrait of a small man, maybe five foot, six inches tall, with a thick, round torso, a sunburned face, and slight traces of gray around the edges of his black hair.

Back at home, he wolfed down the cold beef stew, then shaved and dressed for work in his daily uniform of overalls with rolled-up bottoms, a denim shirt, and black high-top work shoes. His eye patch always went on last. Any time he was working or in public, Jack wore a shop worker's cap. He believed his eye patch was not as prominent when he was wearing the cap. Finally, lunch pail in hand, he went to the back porch and retrieved his bicycle.

Moments later, he was riding across the front yard on the bicycle. As he set upon Highway 17, he saw Frances, wearing a ridiculous-looking black wig, putting out tomato plants.

When she saw Jack, she stood up.

"You want to have supper tonight after you finish the light?"

"Yeah. I'll make sure I'm hungry."

Frances smiled and waved.

For nine years now, Jack had been living across the highway from Frances and, during that time, they had forged a mutually beneficial relationship. Jack, a master mechanic, would fix her car and do odd jobs around the house. The previous year, when a tornado had sent her chicken house tumbling across the pasture, Jack had torn it apart and rebuilt it on the original spot. She offered him $10 for his work, but he said $5 would fine if she would make up the rest in canned peaches and green beans. If Jack needed sewing done or had questions about cooking, he would always go to Frances.

***

Twenty minutes later, Jack was pedaling the three miles to his job at the Cotton States Tire reclamation plant in Hokes Bluff. Although Jack was a master mechanic, he didn't own a car because he was unable to pass the vision test for a license. As he pedaled the bicycle, his thoughts wandered back to his childhood.

Jack had never had a family. Born in a home for unwed mothers in Tuscaloosa, he was put up for adoption only days after his birth. During gestation, Jack's left eye, for whatever reason, didn't develop and, when he was born, his left eye socket was a dark, sunken hole with a tiny, withered eye inside that looked straight up. The iris was filled with a milky-colored liquid and he had no sight in the eye. At age six, Jack was sent to the state orphanage at Montgomery, where he grew up. Intelligent and well-behaved, Jack was a good student and, despite his handicap, he excelled at shop classes and showed a talent for mechanics.

Now, at age 43, Jack had carved out a reasonably normal life for himself.

He worked full-time at the tire reclamation company. Hour after hour, he would use a front-end loader to transport old tires from the company warehouse to an incinerator some fifty yards away. It was a dirty, thankless job, but the supervisor left Jack alone and it paid eighty cents an hour, which was a good salary. Jack had no social life. He never went out to eat or to movies or visit friends other than Miss Hathaway, so, once his simple needs were met, he was able to save a large part of his salary.

Once Jack arrived at the plant, he punched in, fired up the front-end loader, and began work. It was an uneventful day. He hauled thirty-three loads of old tires from the warehouse to the incinerator. Just before lunch, the office secretary brought him a piece of cake. She said the owner was celebrating his birthday and he wanted his employees to enjoy it with him. Jack wolfed down the chocolate cake with relish. That afternoon, he punched out at 5:20, then rode his bicycle back down Highway 17 to his home.

***

Back at home, he changed clothes, had a glass of milk, then went across the street to Frances' house. She greeted him, then together they went to the pantry and Jack inspected the light. After removing two screws, he could see the wire to one terminal had burned through and would have to be shortened, then reattached. Jack set about fixing the light. As Jack worked, Frances watched.

Frances Hathaway was one of those unfortunate women who was doomed to remain forever unmarried. First, she was very tall, every inch of six foot four inches and, when she stood beside most men, she towered over them so much there was no semblance of the two being "a couple." Further, she had a long, horse-like face with a huge, prominent nose. Then there was her hair. When she was in her early twenties, the hair on top of her head began to fall out. Not on the sides, only on top. Once the condition set in, she was almost bald-headed by the time she was twenty-five. For a while, she combed her hair so that the hair on the sides would cover the top, but that looked worse than ever. Finally, she settled for wigs, but it seemed that every hairpiece she bought looked more artificial than the last. Now, at fifty-one, she had retired from a department store over in Hamilton with a small pension and, with a garden, chickens, and a cow, she lived quite comfortably.

Once the defective wire was reattached, Jack replaced the housing, then pulled the switch. The light illuminated the pantry.

Frances smiled.

"Thanks," she said, handing him one dollar.

"Can I get a dozen eggs instead?"

"Sure!"

Ten minutes later, they were seated at the table eating meat loaf, green beans, and mashed potatoes.

"How's the beans?" Frances asked. "Did I get enough salt?"

"Beans are perfect."

They ate quietly for several minutes.

"Do you ever miss not having a family?" Frances said.

"Oh, yeah. Many times," Jack said thoughtfully. "Especially when I was young. When I was three or four, I remember the parents coming to the orphanage every year to see the kids who were up for adoption. They would stop and look at me, see my eye, then quickly move on. Kids on either side of me would get adopted, but nobody wanted me because of my eye."

Jack stopped and dipped more mashed potatoes.

For Love of Daniel

"Didn't that bother you?"

"Of course. I knew the parents wanted a child with two good eyes, but there was nothing I could do. After a few years, I just quit hoping."

They ate quietly.

"I know the feeling," Frances said finally. "When I was a teenager, I dreamed of finding a nice boy and getting married and having a family. All around me, my friends were dating and having weddings and kids, but there was nobody for me. After I turned twenty, I kept thinking I would surely be married by the time I was twenty-five. Then when I was in my late twenties, I thought for sure I would be married by the time I was thirty, but it never happened."

"We have to go on in this world," Jack said finally, helping himself to more meatloaf. "That's all we can do."

"Yeah, maybe you're right. Ready for peach cobbler?"

"Sure."

Moments later, Jack was digging into a bowl of peach cobbler.

Frances watched as he ate.

"They're having all-day singing and dinner on the ground next Sunday at church. You want to go with me and Mildred?"

Frances and her older sister Mildred attended services every Sunday at Old Harmony Baptist.

"No. I think I'll stay home. I've got some things to do."

She peered at him for a long moment.

"Don't you like me?"

"Yes, Miss Hathaway. I like you. Fact is, you're my best friend. I depend on you just like you depend on me, but we shouldn't go spoiling things by getting too serious."

Her head dropped. She looked away without answering.

For Love of Daniel

Visitor

The following morning, Jack was awakened by the roar of high winds and huge sheets of rain pelting the walls and windows of the small clapboard structure. He sat up in bed, threw his feet over the side, and went to the window. To the north, he could see intermittent flashes of lightning followed by bursts of thunder, which rattled the window panes. *It's going to be a miserable ride to work today*, he thought. Quickly, he dressed, went to the kitchen, and took the water bucket to go to the well.

When he opened the front door, he stopped. Huge rivulets of rain were dripping from the roof amid a steady downpour. For a long moment, he waited in the doorway for the rain to slacken, then suddenly, out of the corner of his eye, he noticed a clump of clothing and a suitcase on the porch. Instantly, he was taken aback. He moved closer. Now he could make out the figure of a young woman wearing a flowery head rag and dressed in a heavy men's overcoat. She was asleep. Her back was turned to him. For a long moment, he peered at her without making a move. Then, water bucket in hand, he cautiously moved closer.

"Hello!!" Jack said. "Hello!! Hello!!"

The clump of clothes didn't move.

"Hello!!" Jack said again, louder this time.

The clump of clothes moved slightly and the woman, still half-asleep, turned her face to Jack and opened her eyes. Jack wasn't wearing his eye patch.

"Ooh!" she said, upon seeing Jack.

"Why are you sleeping on my porch?"

The woman sat up and rubbed her eyes. When she sat upright, Jack could see her belly was swollen with child.

"I'm sorry," she said. "I didn't have anywhere to go. My husband and I got into an argument and he pushed me out of the car. This was the nearest house I could find in the rain. I'm sorry. I don't want to be any trouble."

Jack peered at her.

"Your husband left you out in the rain? And you're carrying his child?"

She nodded.

"I don't want to be a problem. I'll just leave."

She slowly started to stand up but, with her heavy belly, Jack could see it was a chore.

"No! No! You don't have to leave. Maybe I can help you. Where is your family?"

She looked at him as if he had said a dirty word.

"Family? What family?"

"You don't have any family?"

"No."

"And your husband? Where is he now?"

"God only knows."

"You don't have anywhere to go? You don't have anyone to help you?"

The woman shook her head.

For Love of Daniel

Jack studied the woman for a moment. Suddenly, the wind shifted and rain began to blow on the porch.

"Well, you can't stay out here. Let's go inside. Let me see if I can help you."

He reached down and offered his hand. She hesitated.

"What happened to your eye?"

"I was born that way."

She grimaced slightly, then took Jack's hand and he pulled her to her feet. Uncertainly, she stood upright and Jack put his arm under hers for support.

"Come on!" he said, taking her suitcase. "Let's go inside."

***

Moments later, the woman was seated on a small couch. Now that she was out of the heavy overcoat and head cloth, Jack could see that she was in her late thirties, petite and pretty with blonde hair, blue eyes, and long legs. Jack made coffee while they chatted.

"What kind of man would leave his pregnant wife out in the rain?"

"You don't know Carl. He goes crazy when he gets mad."

Jack sat a cup of hot coffee on the table in front of her.

She looked at it, then tasted it.

"Do you have a little sugar?"

Jack brought her a small bowl of sugar. He watched as the woman measured a small amount in a teaspoon, dumped it into the cup, then stirred it.

"We left Birmingham last night and were going to Nashville so he could do another show. We stopped in Trussville for a hamburger and got into an argument. He found out I had been with another man and that's when he put me out of the car. He said this child wasn't his."

Jack studied her.

"I don't want to be no trouble," she continued. "If I didn't have this baby, I wouldn't have stopped."

"I can't put you out like this. Not with you being pregnant and all."

Jack inhaled and pondered her dilemma.

"I've got to go to work right now," he said finally. "But you can stay here today. I'll be back this afternoon and we'll figure this out. There's some beef stew and cornbread and fresh milk in the refrigerator. If you want to rest, you can use my bed over there. I don't have time to change the sheets, but I'll get them out and you can do that."

"That's very kind of you. I promise I won't be too much trouble. All I want to do is have this baby and get back on the road."

Over the next twenty minutes, Jack washed, shaved, and put on fresh clothing and his eye patch. Finally, lunch pail in hand, he started out the door.

"Now make yourself at home. I would feel awful if something bad happened to you."

"You go ahead. I'll be just fine. I'll be here when you get in this afternoon."

"By the way," Jack said. "What's your name?"

"My real name is Wanda Sue Smith, but my stage name is Suzanne."

"Stage name?"

For Love of Daniel

"Yes. Suzanne Glamore. I'm an entertainer."

Jack had never known an entertainer before.

"Which do you want me to call you?"

"Suzanne!"

"Okay, Suzanne, my name is Jack. I'll see you this afternoon."

***

Ten minutes later, Jack was pedaling the four miles to the tire reclamation plant. The rain had stopped, but the dirt shoulders of the asphalt road were wet and muddy and Jack had to pedal harder to maintain speed. He felt a certain excitement at the prospect of having a woman in his house. Other than Frances, she was the only woman who had ever been inside. Part of him worried that the woman might have the baby while he was at work. Another part of him worried she might steal something and be gone by the time he returned.

That day, Jack loaded only twenty-eight loads of tires into the incinerator. Usually, he would load more than that, but the intermittent rain and mud had slowed down his productivity. Finally, he punched out at 5:22 that afternoon. During the ride back to his home, he wondered what he would find when he arrived.

When Jack opened the door, the woman was at the sink.

"I changed the sheets on the bed and cleaned up your kitchen a little."

"You didn't have to do all of that."

"I wanted to do something.... You helping me and all."

"When are you supposed to have your baby?"

"Next few days."

"I better go over and get my friend Miss Hathaway. She's a midwife and knows about these things. You stay right here."

"I ain't going nowhere."

***

Fifteen minutes later, Jack reappeared with Frances.

"This is Miss Frances Hathaway."

Suzanne gave her a suspicious smile.

"How many babies you delivered?"

"One hundred four."

Suzanne peered at her.

"I guess you'll do. I don't have much choice."

"When's your due date?"

"Doctor in Birmingham said April 21."

"That's three days away."

Frances studied the woman for a long moment, then turned to Jack.

"I'm going to have to examine her. That way, we can get some idea of what to expect. It would be best if you wait outside while I do this."

"I understand," Jack said. "Just tell me what you need."

Over the next thirty minutes, Jack waited outside while Frances examined the woman. Finally, she came out.

"She's going to have this baby in the next couple days. You going to let her stay here?"

For Love of Daniel

"What else can I do? She hasn't got any family or anywhere to go. Aren't there homes for cases like this?"

"There's the home for unwed mothers in Birmingham, but that's more than eighty miles. We can't move her; she's going to have this baby any day."

Jack peered at her thoughtfully.

"Then we don't have much choice."

Frances nodded.

"Well, we better prepare. Can you let her have the full bed?"

"I can do that. I'll clean out the other room and make myself a palette in there."

***

That night, Frances cooked a meal of fried chicken, black-eyed peas, and boiled potatoes.

"My! My!" Suzanne said as they ate. "I hadn't had any home-cooked food in so long, I'd forgotten what it tastes like. All I ever eat is fast food."

"You're going to have to put lots of nourishment in your body," Frances said. "The baby needs it more than you."

They ate quietly for several minutes.

"What are your plans after having the baby?" Frances said.

"Where I'm going, I'm not going to have time for a baby."

"Where are you going?" Frances said.

"I'm going out to Hollywood to be a movie star. I'm going to have my name in lights and everybody in the whole world is going to know who I am."

Frances cast a furtive glance at Jack.

"What are you going to do with the baby?" Frances asked.

"I don't know. I can't take it with me. I guess I'll put it up for adoption."

A long silence as they ate.

Finally, Suzanne spoke.

"Do y'all want this child? It would be a good thing for the both of you, considering neither one of you has a family."

Jack looked at Frances.

"Do y'all want this child?"

"What about the papers?" Jack asked. "You can't just leave the baby here without any legal documents."

"Why not?" Suzanne continued. "Who would ever know what happened but us? This is not Atlanta. Out here in the country, the authorities don't check on those things like they do in the big cities."

Another long silence as they ate.

"Who is the father?" Frances asked.

Suzanne hesitated.

"I'm not sure. It might be Bill's. Then again, the father could be a man I met who was on his way to Texas. We spent a couple nights together in Birmingham."

"I thought you were married," Jack said.

"No, not really," Suzanne continued. "Me and Carl told everybody we were married for appearances' sake, but we never were. Chances are, if the truth be told, it's Carl's baby."

"He doesn't want the baby?"

She laughed.

For Love of Daniel

"Carl has got even less need for a baby than I do."

A long silence.

"Well, you're going to have the baby first," Frances said finally. "We really can't decide anything until you have the baby."

***

Over the next two days, the mother-to-be stayed at Jack's house and slept in his bed. Both days, while Jack worked, Frances would come in and cook and clean and prepare for the birth. She had brought some old loose-fitting clothes for Suzanne to wear and counselled her to rest, stay quiet, and drink plenty of milk. Also, she had gone into town and stocked up on cloth diapers, baby oil, and powder.

"I've got a little opium the doctor gave me," she said. "When you start to dilate, I'll give you some. It will make the birth a lot easier."

***

On the afternoon of the second day, Jack was dog-tired when he pedaled the bicycle into the front yard. Frances was sitting on the front porch.

"How's she doing?" Jack asked.

"She's asleep right now. She's going to have that baby tonight."

"Is everything ready?"

"I've done all I know to do."

"Then we'll have to wait."

Daniel

That night, Jack was suddenly awakened from a sound sleep by loud screams. At first, he trembled at the sound.

"Push!! Push!" he could hear Frances saying in the other room. "Push! Push with all your might!"

Then there was another loud scream and still another.

Suddenly, the screaming stopped, then there was the sound of a baby crying. The sound sent cold shivers up Jack's spine. Moments later, he was out of bed and in the living room. There he found Frances sitting on the couch rocking a newborn infant in a blanket.

"It's a little boy. And he's a fine one."

For a brief moment, Jack pulled back the edge of the blanket and peered at the sleeping child. Curiously, he used his index finger to feel the soft skin on the baby's arm. At his touch, the child opened its eyes, yawned, and looked straight into Jack's eyes. Still holding Jack's eye, the infant's tiny hand reached out and grasped Jack's finger. Jack started to pull the finger away, but the child clung tenaciously to the finger, so Jack ceased trying to pull it away. The infant continued clutching the finger, then moments later, dozed off to sleep again and released the finger.

Jack smiled happily.

Then he turned back to Frances.

"How's the mother?"

For Love of Daniel

"She's still asleep. She's going to need to rest for a day or two."

Jack didn't reply.

Frances peered at him.

"If she leaves this baby, do you think me and you could take care of it?"

Jack shook his head.

"I'm not sure. It would mean a big change in our lives. Both of our lives."

"Together we could do it. If we organized and planned."

"What about the papers?" Jack asked.

"What about the papers? If we go into town and tell them what happened, they might take the baby away. If we don't say anything, who is going to ask?"

Frances peered at the infant.

"It would be nice to have a child in my life. Wouldn't you like to have a child?"

Jack studied her for a long moment.

"Yes," he said finally.

***

The next morning, Jack was up early. When he went into the living room, Frances was asleep on the couch. As quickly and as quietly as possible, Jack prepared a lunch, washed, shaved, and left for work.

When Suzanne awoke around noon, Frances was waiting with a bowl of chicken soup.

"How you feeling?"

"I'm weak," Suzanne said, sipping the soup. "I need a little time to get my strength back, then I'm going to be gone."

"You've got to stay for a while to nurse this baby."

"How long will that be?"

"Couple or three weeks at least."

"I can't be here that long."

Suzanne finished the soup and handed the bowl back.

"You got a set of bathroom scales?"

"I think I got some in the garage," Frances replied. "I'll have to check."

***

Over the next two days, Frances spent more time at Jack's house than she did her own. In the mornings, before Jack left for work, she would appear and start cooking, cleaning, and washing. One moment, she was counselling Suzanne about giving herself time to recover, then she was changing diapers, supervising nursing, and attending to the baby while Suzanne slept. She had bought an alarm clock so Suzanne could nurse the baby every four hours and a set of bathroom scales.

The moment Suzanne saw the scales, she had to try them.

"My Lord!" she said. "I weigh 123 pounds. I'm going to have to lose some weight before I can go back on the chorus line."

On the third day after the birth, Suzanne said she couldn't stay in bed any longer. Once she was up, she had breakfast, popped open her suitcase, and spread out an array of clothes, shoes, movie star magazines, and an assortment of lipstick, makeup, and fingernail polish. Frances watched curiously as Suzanne applied makeup and lipstick. Once Suzanne was finished, she squeezed herself into a pair of tight blue jeans, slipped on some tennis shoes, and announced she was going for a walk.

"I need to exercise. I got to get back to a size 6."

She was gone for almost an hour.

"My goodness, this is the backwoods around here. What do y'all do for fun?"

"What do you mean?"

"Don't you ever party or go to the movies or just hang out with your friends at the local diner?"

Frances smiled.

"There's too much work to do. We don't have time."

Suzanne shook her head.

"I couldn't live like this. I would go crazy with boredom."

***

Over the next few days, Suzanne occupied herself with walking, doing her nails, and reading the Sears and Roebuck catalog while Frances attended to the baby. At night, Frances would cook and counselled Suzanne she needed to eat.

One night, when Jack arrived home, Frances had another home-cooked meal waiting. Once they sat down to eat, Suzanne turned to Frances.

"You do a good job being a mama. Much better than me. What are y'all going to call him?"

"We can name him?" Frances said.

"Sure! This baby belongs to y'all as far as I'm concerned."

Frances glanced at Jack, then back to Suzanne.

"Are you truly and honestly going to leave this baby with us?"

"Yes. I'm serious as a heart attack. Don't you believe me?"

Frances looked to Jack. He was helping himself to more mashed potatoes.

A long silence.

"So I'll ask you again. What are y'all going to call him?"

"We'll name him Daniel," Frances said finally. "After the man in the Bible God saved from the lion's den."

"You going to call him Daniel Griffin?"

"We'll call him Daniel Jackson Griffin," Jack said.

"That's a nice name," Suzanne replied.

Once the meal was finished, Frances put away the food, washed dishes, and counselled Suzanne she needed to wake up just around midnight to nurse the baby. Once Frances had gone home for the night, Suzanne and Jack sat on the front porch in the darkness and sipped iced tea. From the nearby river, they could hear a chorus of bullfrogs.

A long silence.

"Frogs are louder than usual tonight," Jack said finally. "I think it's because of the full moon."

Suzanne laughed.

"A full moon will make frogs croak louder?"

"That's right."

"I never heard that," she said, still chuckling. "Y'all people in these hills are just full of wisdom."

For Love of Daniel

They were quiet again. The bullfrogs croaked away. Finally, Jack spoke.

"Can I ask you a question?"

"Sure."

"You think a woman like you could ever be interested in a man like me?"

Suzanne peered curiously at him in the darkness.

"Are you sweet on me?"

"Maybe.... a little. I was just wondering."

"I could never fall for a man like you. We're too different. Way, way too different."

"With this eye patch, I'm not much to look at, but I'm a hard worker, I'm honest, and I try to be a good person."

Suzanne laughed.

"You ever been married, Jack?"

"No."

"Have you ever been with a woman?"

"Yeah. A few times."

Suzanne inhaled, then turned back to him.

"Where I'm going, you would never fit in. Out in Hollywood, you've got to be perfect. What's more, you're too old."

"I'm not all that old. I'm forty-three, six years older than you."

"If I was in Hollywood and people saw me with you, they would say 'what's that beautiful woman doing with that one-eyed man?'"

"When I wear my patch, it don't look all that bad."

"It's pretty bad. You would never pass in Hollywood."

A long silence as Jack sipped his iced tea.

"And you ain't got nothing," Suzanne continued. "I'll bet you don't even own this house."

"No, I don't. I rent, but I work and I keep the rent paid."

Another long silence.

"Don't feel bad, Jack. Men fall in love with me all the time. All I got to do is snap my fingers and men come crawling."

Jack studied her.

"But I appreciate the offer. You and Frances have been really nice to me and I am thankful."

Suddenly, they heard the baby crying.

Suzanne got up.

"I got to go in now and nurse the baby."

***

The following afternoon, when Jack came home from work, Suzanne was alone with the baby. When he walked in, he saw a huge poster of a chorus line on the wall. The caption read "Naughty Girls!" and featured a line of scantily-dressed, lace-stockinged women kicking their heels in the air.

When Jack saw it, he stopped.

"I hope you don't mind me putting up my poster."

"That's fine."

"See the fourth girl from the left?" Suzanne said, getting up to indicate. "That's me! Don't you think I'm beautiful?"

Jack looked at the poster.

"Oh yes. Very pretty."

For Love of Daniel

"The one on the end, the brunette, that's Doris. She's my best friend."

"Very pretty."

Jack turned to go to the bedroom.

"I'm going to change clothes."

"When's the amazon coming over?"

Jack peered at her for a long moment.

"She'll be here. She said she was going to cook tonight."

***

Two hours later, the three of them sat down to a vegetable dinner.

"Is beans and potatoes and cornbread all y'all ever eat around here? Don't you ever have filet mignon or potatoes au gratin?"

"This is not the Ritz," Frances said. "We're poor folks."

Suzanne shook her head in frustration.

"My Lord, I could never live back in these sticks. Y'all are out here in the middle of nowhere. No stores, no theaters. No restaurants. I couldn't spend my nights listening to the frogs."

"Sometimes we listen to the radio," Jack said.

Suzanne laughed.

"Well, whoop de-do! You ain't even got a television. Y'all know there's a big wide world out there. Right?"

"We're just simple country folks," Jack said.

Suzanne laughed again.

"And an outhouse. I hadn't used an outhouse since I was a little girl visiting my grandmother down in

Macon. Oh, Lord, I'll never forget the smell. This kind of living is for country folks. I'm a city girl myself."

Jack looked at Frances.

They ate quietly.

"Jack, can you do me favor?" Suzanne said. "Can you move your patch a little to the left? I can still see inside that blank eye of yours."

Jack looked at Frances.

She nodded slightly.

Instantly, Jack got up from the table and went to the mirror and adjusted the patch.

"Is that better?" he asked, returning to the table.

"A little better," Suzanne replied. "I can still see part of the inside, but I guess it will be okay now."

Jack looked at Frances. She didn't answer.

***

That night, after Suzanne and the baby were asleep, Jack and Frances sat on the front porch in the darkness listening to the frogs.

"I'm going to the church singing with Mildred on Sunday. Do you think you and Suzanne and the baby will be okay for a couple of hours?"

"We'll be fine. Have you told Mildred about the baby?"

"No. I'm going to wait."

"How long? You know when she finds out, she's going to have something to say. Your sister goes by the book."

"I know. I'm going to wait until the time is right."

For Love of Daniel

Exodus

A week passed. All that time, Suzanne was becoming more and more restless. In the mornings, decked out in blue jeans and tennis shoes, she would walk the two miles to the Burma Shave sign on Highway 17, then back to Jack's house. Every day, after returning from her walk, Suzanne would quiz Frances about her appearance.

"How do I look? Can you tell I've lost weight?"

"You're thinner than you were."

"Do I look like the woman in the poster?"

Frances glanced at the poster, then back at Suzanne.

"Pretty close."

You're not lying, are you?" Suzanne said. "Just to be agreeable?"

"Why would I lie about it?"

***

One morning, Frances came early to check on the child, then, satisfied everything was okay, she returned to her house. That afternoon, she heard the baby crying. Instantly, she went back across the highway.

When Frances entered the house, the baby was still wailing and Suzanne was on the floor doing sit-ups.

"Don't you hear that baby?" Frances asked.

"Yeah, I hear it, but I don't know what to do. I don't know nothing about babies."

Frances went to the child.

Moments later, the baby was quiet again.

"What's was wrong?" Suzanne asked.

"A diaper pin was sticking it."

"I would never know to check for something like that."

Frances studied her for a moment.

"Don't you have any feelings for this baby?"

"Yeah. I have feelings for it. I wouldn't want to see anything happen to it, but I can't honestly say I love it. I don't need it. I've got too many other things in my life."

Frances studied her for a moment.

"How did you grow up?" she asked. "What kind of parents did you have?"

"My parents were divorced when I was three and I was raised by my father and my stepmother. My daddy owned a hotel on Atlanta's east side and he ran women. My daddy abused me and treated me like the women he ran. To my daddy, all women were split-tails. Me included. That's why I ran away from home when I was fifteen."

"Sounds like you didn't have much of a childhood. Is that why you're so cold-hearted?"

Suzanne stopped at the word.

"Cold-hearted? Is that what I am?"

She peered thoughtfully at Frances.

"Yeah. I guess you could say I'm cold-hearted. That's how you become when you're raised like I was. You get hard or you don't survive. That's one thing I learned from my daddy. He used to say: 'If you don't

For Love of Daniel

take care of number one, nobody else will.' He said that's the only way to make it in this world. Yeah. I'm cold-hearted because I have had to survive."

Frances didn't reply.

"And that's what's going to make me a star out in Hollywood. I'm going to do whatever I have to do to make it. They say that all a pretty girl has to do is give it up and those producers will make a big star out of you."

"You've already given it up a few times."

"Yeah," Suzanne replied. "I guess you could say that. I like to enjoy myself. I am a natural woman."

Frances studied her for a long moment.

"You're a Jezebel."

Instantly, livid anger flashed across Suzanne's face

"A Jezebel? You calling me a whore? That's easy for you to say! Look at me! I can get a man. You can't!!"

Instantly, she was in Frances' face.

"Did you hear what I said? I'm not like you. My hole is not dry. I can get a man!"

Itching for a fight, she grabbed Frances' arm.

"Are you listening to me?"

Instantly, Frances slapped her hand away.

"I heard what you said."

Suzanne, fire in her eyes, wasn't finished.

"You think because I'm staying here with y'all, you can call me names and insult me? I know what you holier-than-thou Christian types are all about. You go judging people with your Bible stories. Hypocrites! That's what you are! All of you are just a bunch of hypocrites. Do you hear me?"

When Frances didn't respond right away, Suzanne grew even angrier.

"Do you hear me?" she shouted. "Hypocrites! That's all you are!"

Frances, calmer now, backed away.

"I'm sorry. I shouldn't have said it."

"That's right. You shouldn't have said it. Your mouth is bigger than your brain. You got any more questions?"

Frances peered at her.

"Yeah. Why are you so mean to Jack?"

"You mean about his eye patch and all?"

"Yes. He's very sensitive about it."

"I wasn't being mean. I was just telling the truth."

"Some things are better left unsaid."

"Not for me. The truth never hurt nobody."

***

At the end of that week, Suzanne was fit to be tied.

"I can't stay here any longer," she said over dinner one night. "I've got to get back on the chorus line. I want to know if y'all will help me."

"What do you need?" Jack said.

"First, I need to make some phone calls."

"I have a phone," Frances said. "You can use it to make whatever calls you want."

"They're long-distance. To Nashville and Birmingham. And I don't have any money."

"That's okay," Frances said. "I'll be glad to help you."

For Love of Daniel

They ate quietly.

"And I need a couple new dresses. I saw some nice ones in the Sears and Roebuck catalog."

"Pick out the ones you want and I'll pay for them," Jack said.

"Thanks! Y'all been really nice to me."

The following morning, Suzanne showed Jack and Frances the dresses she wanted. Frances called in the order so the dresses would arrive faster.

***

Over the next few days, Suzanne prepared for her exodus. Every morning, she would put on jeans and tennis shoes and walk the two miles from Jack's house along the highway to the Burma Shave sign and back. At night, over the objections of Frances, she ate little or nothing and spent the days reading movie star magazines, chatting with Frances, and primping.

On Friday of that week, over dinner with Jack and Frances, she announced she was back to a size 6.

"When my new dresses get here, I'll be gone."

The two dresses arrived in the mail the following Thursday. Since Jack didn't have a full-length mirror, Suzanne went to Frances' house to try them on. She was happy with the fit and, after trying on several pairs of shoes, she found some she felt matched the dresses.

That afternoon, she made long-distance calls to Nashville and Birmingham on Frances' phone.

Frances sat in the living room and listened.

"It's the first farm on the left after the Burma Shave sign. There will be a red barn on the left side of the road with a 'See Rock City' sign. You can't miss it."

A pause.

"10:30 tomorrow? Okay. I'll be waiting."

***

Over dinner that night, she announced to Jack and Frances that she was leaving the following morning.

"We're going to need some information for the birth certificate," Jack said.

"What kind of information?"

"What's your real name?" Jack asked.

"My real name is Wanda Sue Smith from Decatur, Ga. I was born Sept. 9, 1918. If anybody wants to be sure of my identity, I've got a heart-shaped tattoo on my right arm."

She pulled up her sleeve to show them the tattoo.

"That tattoo is what police call an 'identifying characteristic.' I guess you could say it's mine. What else do you want to know?"

"Who should we put down as the father?" Jack asked.

"Yourself. I don't know who the real father is."

Jack and Frances looked ominously at one another.

"Anything else? Suzanne asked.

"Will we ever hear from you again?"

"Probably not."

***

The next morning, Jack was up early and went to work. At 10:30, Frances, the baby, and Suzanne, decked out in one of her new dresses, were waiting on the front porch at Frances' home, when a new Ford sedan pulled into the yard.

"Well, I guess this is good-bye," Suzanne said, picking up her suitcase. "I want to thank you and Jack for helping me."

"We were happy to do it."

Suzanne took a letter out of her purse.

"Give this to Jack."

Frances took the letter.

Suzanne turned to the baby.

"Oh, little Daniel. I wish you well in this world. These people will love you and take care of you because your mama sure can't. Especially at this time in my life. So I'm leaving you with these people, knowing that you will be safe and in good hands."

Then she kissed the baby on the forehead and gave Frances an awkward hug.

"Please take care of Daniel."

Moments later, she went down the steps and got into the waiting car. As the vehicle pulled out on the highway, Suzanne waved good-bye one last time.

"If you want to write, send me a letter addressed to Suzanne Glamore, Hollywood California. I'll get it."

Then she waved again. Frances watched as the sedan sped off down the highway.

***

That night, Jack read Suzanne's letter.

Dear Jack:
Thanks for all the things you and Frances did for me. I don't know how I would have made it without y'all.

John I. Jones

I wanted to tell you that I took $200 out of your stash in the shed. I knew you had money hidden out there when you went to get the money for the COD for the dresses. I know you won't miss it. That will buy me a bus ticket to Los Angeles and living expenses for a while. By then, I'll be a big star and I'll pay you back. As for the baby, he belongs to you and that amazon woman that lives across the street. I don't have time to go before a judge and declare myself the mother of that baby and sign a bunch of papers. I know y'all will love that child and take care of him. I wish y'all the best. Thanks for everything.

Suzanne.

Jack folded the letter thoughtfully then went to the bedroom and placed it inside an old shoe box where he kept important papers. Then he went outside to the tool shed in the back yard. Inside, he reached down a fruit jar where he kept cash. Last time he had checked, there was just over $200 inside. It was empty. Instantly, he went to the corner of the shed and pulled a heavy canvas cloth from atop an old planting plow. Then he reached inside and withdrew another fruit jar. He opened it and counted the money.

There was $723 inside. All of the money was still there. Quickly, he replaced the lid and returned the jar to its hiding place, then left the shed and started across the highway to Frances' house.

Mildred

Ten minutes later, Jack was across the highway at Frances' house. When he walked in, Daniel was asleep.

"Sit down," she said. "We need to talk."

Jack took a seat on the sofa.

"It would be best if Daniel lives with me. I can't be running across the highway at midnight to feed him or change his diaper. I've got indoor plumbing and more room, so he can spread out as he grows."

"That's fine."

"Also, we're going to need a few things. A cradle, a stroller, and a high chair. Also, we're going to have to get a goat."

"A goat?"

"Yes. This baby has got to have fresh milk every day at least for a few more weeks. Remember, his mother is not here anymore."

"I'll see what I can do. Is that everything?"

"For now."

Frances studied him for a moment.

"Jack, do you think we can raise this child?"

"I don't see why not. We'll have to be organized and work together, but I believe we can do it."

She smiled.

"Yes. I believe we can too."

"Now you're the expert in these things," he continued. "Just tell me what I need to do and I'll do it."

John I. Jones

"Thanks, Jack. Thanks so much!!"

***

The following morning, a Saturday, Jack, Frances, and the baby loaded up in Frances' car and went into Hokes Bluff to the second-hand store.

"Frances!" Mrs. Henderson, the store proprietor, said upon seeing the infant. "Is this your new baby?"

"Oh, no, he's not my child. This is a nephew of mine. I'll be keeping him for a while."

"That's nice," Mrs. Henderson said. "Babies always brighten up a household."

Over the next thirty minutes, they found a cradle for two dollars and a high chair with a broken leg. Once Jack had inspected it, he said he could fix it and Frances offered one dollar. The woman accepted.

When Frances asked about strollers, the proprietor said they didn't have any in stock at the moment. After Jack spotted an old used stroller with two wheels missing, he asked about it.

"Oh, that old thing," the woman said. "That's from the thirties. It's still got the white ceramic handles. You wouldn't want that."

Frances looked at Jack.

"I can fix it," he said.

"I'll give you a dollar," Frances said.

"Sold!"

Before they left, Frances also bought two baby blankets, an electric bottle warmer, and some used baby clothes.

Once the goods were loaded, they were driving back home.

For Love of Daniel

"Now that's the story we're going to tell," Frances said. "If anybody wants to know how we got this baby, we're going to tell them he's my nephew and we're going to be keeping him for a while."

"What if people ask where your sister lives or her name?"

"You don't have to provide too many details. Just say it's my nephew and leave it at that. Can you remember that?"

"I'll remember."

That afternoon, Jack rode his bicycle over to a farm near Hamilton and bought a goat. Since Jack had no way to transport the animal, he paid the farmer to deliver it to Frances' farm.

***

By the end of the first week, Jack and Frances had laid the groundwork for their great adventure. Before leaving for work every day, Jack would stop at Frances' house and check on her and Daniel. If she needed grocery items, Jack would make a list and pick them up on his way home. Once he arrived home, he went directly to Frances' house and provided her some "relief," as she called it. Frances taught Jack how to milk the goat and strain and boil the milk before it was fed to the baby. Very quickly, he became quite expert at warming baby bottles, changing diapers, and burping the infant.

Over the next few weeks, again and again, Frances found herself consulting *Miss Busby's Original Guide to Midwifery*, her long-time personal Bible on the subject. She had delivered over a hundred children, but she had never faced the task of raising one. As a result, she had to bone up on all of the dos and don'ts of infant care. The child had to have a rigid feeding schedule; his bottle had to be warmed to just the right temperature; the child's sleeping environment had to be just so; the list was endless. Also, Frances, an avid newspaper and magazine reader, found herself constantly clipping and saving articles on infant care.

On Saturday mornings, which they dubbed "diaper day," Jack would get up early and build a fire around the old wash pot in Frances' backyard. Once the diapers were boiled and clean, Jack would fish them out, place them in a wicker basket, then hold the basket while Frances strung the wet diapers along a clothesline. After he had repaired the leg on the high chair, Jack bought the materials and made a cradle. He painted it light baby blue and, in darker blue on either side, he stenciled the word "Daniel." At his work, Jack found an old toy wagon in a storage shed, which had wheels that perfectly matched those on the stroller. He asked if he could have it. Once the supervisor approved, Jack took the wagon home and placed all four wheels on the old baby stroller. Frances was delighted.

By the end of the first month, Jack and Frances were on a firm schedule. Jack continued to work and Frances divided up her time between Daniel and her farm duties. Jack already had his own garden well underway, but Frances, due to the additional time she was spending with the baby, asked Jack to help with hers. She asked him to string pole beans and make tomato beds. Also, there was a leak in the barn roof and she asked that he repair it. He was happy to oblige.

For Love of Daniel

***

By late May, Jack and Frances had had Daniel for a month. Daniel was a good baby. If he was crying, she could rest assured something was wrong. His diaper needed changing, he was hungry, a safety pin was sticking him. He was not the kind of child who cried for no reason. After the first month, he began to sleep through the night without crying. And he was a very active child. Sometimes, early in the morning, he would awaken early and Frances would hear him jabbering to himself. She would get up and go to the crib and, upon seeing her, Daniel would kick and make noise until Frances picked him up.

One afternoon when Jack came in from work, Frances announced it was time to tell Mildred.

"We're becoming very attached to this child. We need to have some idea of where we stand."

"What if she wants to take the child away?"

Frances took a deep breath.

"I'm going to try to convince her not to. We can't hide it from her forever. She's my sister."

"I guess you're right."

***

The next morning, a Saturday, a late model sedan pulled up in the front yard at Frances' farmhouse and a middle-aged, smartly-dressed woman got out. Mildred Gibson was tall for a woman, almost six feet, but she didn't strike the amazon appearance of her younger sister. Dressed in a gray business suit, she was in her late fifties and had been widowed for several years. She had married young and had three children, two of which now had families of their own. Her youngest child, Andy, had been killed in an auto accident as a teenager. For over twenty years now, she had been the director of children's welfare services in Tallapoosa County. As a public servant, she was a member of the Tallapoosa County's auxiliary police force. She had arrest powers and she knew how to shoot a gun.

"Oh, baby sister!" Mildred said upon getting out of the car. "How you been doing?"

Frances leaned her towering frame down to hug her older sister.

"I'm doing fine."

Mildred turned to Jack.

"Hi, Jack!!"

"Morning, Mildred."

"So what is this surprise you want to show me?" Mildred said.

"Come on in," Frances replied.

Inside, Frances led Mildred to the second bedroom.

Instantly, Mildred was taken aback upon she saw the sleeping baby.

"My God!" she said. "A baby? Where did you get a baby?"

Frances explained what happened.

"What are you going to do with it?"

"Me and Jack are going to raise it."

"Baby sister, are you out of your mind? You can't keep this child!"

"Why not? You know I've always wanted a child."

For Love of Daniel

"Yeah, but not like this. This is not the way you do it."

The two sisters studied one another for a moment, then Mildred turned back to the cradle.

"He's a beautiful little boy."

"If it's at all possible," Frances said, "I'm going to keep this child. Jack wants him too."

"In the eyes of the law, you don't have a legal claim. Since the child was abandoned, he should be put into an orphanage."

"He'll never get the kind of love in an orphanage he'll get from me and Jack. What do I have to do to get a legal claim? Can I adopt him?"

"You could, but that's a long process. You would have to get approval from the proper authorities and have legal papers drawn. Also, since you're a single woman, it might be impossible."

"What if the mother is nowhere to be found?"

Mildred shook her head in indecision.

"You would still have to go through the legal process."

Mildred stopped. She still couldn't believe it.

"Are you two really serious about this?"

Frances was unflinching.

"We're dead serious."

Mildred turned to Jack.

"And you're going to help her raise this child?"

"Yes. I've always wanted a child to care for. Neither one of us have ever had a family."

Mildred took a deep breath, looked from one to the other, then back at the child. She shook her head.

"This is just too strange. Too crazy. What do you want me to do?"

"I want you to tell us what we have to do to keep this child," Frances said.

"I've told you," Mildred said. "Sooner or later, you'll have to prove you have a legal right."

Mildred looked from Jack to Frances.

"You know it's my job to report cases like this."

"I know that," Frances said. "Suppose we went ahead and raised the child and you never said anything? Couldn't you make an exception? For me?"

"Oh, my God, I know how much you've always wanted a child."

Mildred looked from one to the other.

"I could lose my job if I don't report it."

"I know," Frances said. "You couldn't do it for me?"

Mildred shook her head indecisively.

"I guess I could just look the other way. I could pretend I didn't know anything about this child."

"Who's going to know?" Frances said.

"But if somebody else brings attention to it, I've got to enforce the law."

"Oh, Mildred!" Frances said. "It would mean so much to me and Jack."

"I'll protect you as long as I can," Mildred said. "But if a third party brings it to my attention, I'll have to file a case."

"Thanks!" Frances said. "I knew I could depend on you."

"Thanks!" Jack said.

"As far as I'm concerned, I don't know anything about this child. We'll let it ride and we'll see what happens. But I wouldn't be advertising the fact that you

For Love of Daniel

have him. The more people who know about him, the more people who can start asking questions."

"I know," Frances said. "We'll keep it quiet."

Mildred was still peering into the crib.

"He's such a beautiful child."

Raising Daniel

So with renewed confidence they could escape with raising Daniel as their own, Jack and Frances continued their great adventure.

One spring morning, three days after Daniel celebrated his first birthday, Frances was washing dishes at the sink and Daniel was playing in a nearby playpen Jack had made. The child was making baby talk and banging a plastic toy hammer on the sides of the playpen.

Frances turned to him and smiled.

"Hey, baby," she said.

Daniel looked up and smiled.

"Mama! Mama!" he suddenly blurted out. Then he banged the plastic hammer on the sides of the playpen. "Mama! Mama!"

Frances stopped. Her eyes filled with tears. She never dreamed she would ever hear those words directed to her.

She went to the playpen, picked up the child, and clutched it to her breast.

"Mama! Mama!" the child said again and again. "Mama! Mama!"

***

For Love of Daniel

One night after dinner at Frances' house, Jack was sitting on the front porch sipping iced tea and listening to the frogs.

"Jack!" Frances called.

Immediately, Jack went inside and found Frances and Daniel on the living room floor. The child was playing with several magazines scattered about the floor.

"Watch this!" Frances said.

She gathered several magazines nearest the child and placed them several feet away. Instantly, Daniel's face screwed up with annoyance. Then, he stood up, took several halting steps to the magazines, and sat down again.

Jack burst out in joyful laughter.

Then Frances, giggling with delight, again moved the magazines away from the child. Again, he stood up, took several steps to the magazines, then plopped to the floor on his bottom again.

"He's walking," Jack said.

Frances shook her head with pure amazement and joy.

***

As he grew older, Jack and Frances could see that Daniel was going to grow up to be an alert, curious child. With deep blue eyes and a headful of blonde curly hair, he was highly intelligent and interested in anything and everything.

"I want to keep this child busy," Frances said. "Idle hands are the devil's workshop."

With Daniel, Frances now had a way of sharing her knowledge and education with a small child. That had always been a dream of hers. So only days after his second birthday, she ordered children's books, a small blackboard, and educational games out of the Sears and Roebuck catalog. She taught him the ABC song, his numbers, and how to spell simple words. Day after day, she worked with him. She taught him to color, draw, and finger-paint. One of his favorite activities was singing children's songs. Once Daniel had heard a song a few times, he quickly memorized it and, at night, long after he was supposed to be asleep, Frances would hear him in his room singing "Mary had a Little Lamb" and "Old McDonald had a Farm."

Frances, an expert seamstress, had an old pedal-powered sewing machine and she made Daniel's shirts out of flour sacks. Each time she bought flour at the grocery, she would check the pattern to be sure she had a different one. Then, back at home, she would measure and snip and sew together the shirts.

***

When he turned three, Frances began to give him chores. First, she taught him to bring the chickens into the henhouse for the night. In the afternoons, when Daniel saw Frances take the milk bucket from the side cupboard, he knew she was going to milk the cow, and instantly, in his black baseball cap, white shirt, and blue denim overalls, he would fall in lockstep behind her.

Before she started milking, she would send him into the nearby field with a small container of crushed corn. Once the chickens heard the child's tapping on the

For Love of Daniel

side of the metal container, they would instantly stop whatever they were doing and come running. The child would scatter a tiny bit of the corn on the ground, then head back to the chicken enclosure behind the barn. Instantly, the chickens would gobble down what feed was on the ground, then run after the child. Once all of the birds were inside the enclosure, Daniel would dump the remainder of the corn into a feed trough. Finally, as the farm fowl ate, Daniel would gather the eggs then lock the door behind him for the night.

"Look, Mama!" he would say proudly, displaying the eggs. "Look at all the eggs I found."

"My! My!" Frances would say. "You're such a big boy! We'll have plenty of eggs for breakfast."

***

For his fourth birthday, Frances put together a birthday party with cake, ice cream, and presents. In attendance were Jack, Frances, and Mildred, and the excited child couldn't wait to open his presents. Jack had bought a wind-up bulldozer and some toy dump trucks. Frances had bought clothes while Mildred had bought several children's books and a toy bubble maker. After the party, Frances and Mildred sat on the front porch and watched Daniel as he played in the front yard. He would dip the plastic hoop into the slippery liquid, then blow bubbles in the air. After marveling for a few seconds, he would run after them and, at just the right moment, gleefully pop them with his finger. At one point, as Mildred watched, she made a startling observation.

"I'll swear, Daniel is the spitting image of Andy," she said, referring to her late son.

Frances nodded.

"He does look a lot like Andy."

"It's scary," Mildred continued. "When I see him running across the yard, it's almost like Andy has come back to earth."

Frances peered at her sister.

Mildred's face was white as a sheet.

"Oh, God! Oh my God!" she said.

"What's wrong?"

"Look at him!"

"What is it?" France asked again.

"Look at the way he runs! The way he holds his head! It's Andy! I tell you, it's him! Andy has been sent back to me! God has sent Andy back to me!"

Suddenly, Mildred burst into tears of joy. For a moment, she sobbed uncontrollably as Frances watched helplessly. Frances had not seen her sister cry since she was a small child.

Moments later, Daniel, finished playing with the bubble maker, bounded onto the porch.

"Come give your Aunt Mildred a hug!" Mildred said.

Dutifully, the child went to her and hugged her.

"Thanks for the bubble maker. I love you, Aunt Mildred."

"I love you too, baby."

Daniel pulled back and looked at her.

"Why have you been crying?"

"I don't know," she said, wiping her eyes.

For Love of Daniel

"Don't cry, Aunt Mildred," he said, patting her shoulder. "It's okay. Don't cry! Everything is going to be all right."

Mildred looked at Frances, pure joy in her face, then turned back at Daniel.

"My! My! You're such a fine boy!"

***

Over the next year, Daniel became Jack's shadow. Everything Jack did, Daniel thought he had to do it. While building a new floor for the back porch, Daniel watched closely as Jack put a piece of lumber on a saw horse, then cut it to the desired length with a handsaw. Once the piece had been cut, Daniel wanted to try it himself. Although Daniel's hand was much too small for the saw's handle, Jack placed the tiny hand inside it, wrapped his own hand around the child's, and went through the motions of cutting the new piece. Once cut, Daniel, his face swelling with pride, looked to Jack for approval.

"Good job!!" Jack said.

Jack was always making toys for Daniel. He would spend endless hours carving little wood figures of men and animals for Daniel to play with. In the backyard at Frances' house, Jack built a spinning jenny. Hour after hour, he and Daniel, whose short legs could barely touch the ground, would spin round and round on the contraption, all the while Daniel squealing with pure joy. Sunday afternoons would always find Jack and Daniel in the backyard at Frances' house playing ball or catching lightning bugs or flying a kite. If Jack wasn't at work, Daniel was at his side.

***

One spring day, Jack took Daniel fishing for the first time at the river behind his house. Together, they dug bait. Jack spaded up huge shovelfuls of dirt behind the shed and Daniel, unafraid of the rapidly wiggling creatures, got down on his knees, gathered the earthworms, and placed them in a tin can. Then Jack rigged up cane poles. Once they arrived at the fishing hole, Jack showed Daniel how to put the worm on the hook and adjust the float. When Daniel caught his first fish, he squealed with pure delight. That day, they caught eleven hand-sized bream.

Upon arriving home, Daniel presented the fresh fish to Frances.

"Look, Mama!"

"Oh, my!!" she said. "Did you catch these?"

"Yep," he said proudly. "Will you cook them for supper?"

"I sure will."

***

Every Christmas, Daniel couldn't wait to receive presents from his "Aunt Mildred." She always bought expensive presents, gifts that Jack and Frances couldn't afford and, when her car pulled into the yard on his fifth Christmas, Daniel went bounding down the porch steps to meet her.

"Aunt Mildred! What did you get me?"

Once inside, he quickly began opening gifts. The first one he opened was a toy football. The moment he

For Love of Daniel

pulled the inflatable football out of its box, his first reaction was "We don't have any way to blow it up."

"You haven't opened all of your presents," Mildred said.

Daniel looked at her and smiled. The additional presents included a needle and a tire pump for inflating the football.

"My Aunt Mildred thinks of everything," Daniel said.

"Your Aunt Mildred is very thorough," Jack said.

"She likes to see things get done," Frances said. "And done right."

Twenty minutes later, the football was inflated and Jack and Daniel were in the front yard tossing it back and forth. In later years, it would prove to be a gift that would change Daniel's life.

When Mildred left that day, Daniel went to her and gave her a hug.

"Thanks for the football," he said. "I love you, Aunt Mildred."

"I love you too, baby."

John I. Jones

The Accident

At the age of five, fishing in the river on Saturdays had become a ritual for Jack and Daniel. When Jack arrived home from work on Fridays, Daniel announced he wanted to go fishing the following morning. One Saturday morning in the early fall of 1960, Jack and Daniel were preparing to go fishing. While Jack rigged the lines, Daniel went behind the shed to dig bait. The container he was using for bait was a small tin can with the jagged edge of its lid still attached. Once the can was filled with earthworms, Daniel went running back around the side of the shed, carrying the bait in the tin can. As he rounded the corner, he slipped and fell and the tin lid of the can cut a nasty gash across his right cheek. Instantly, when Jack saw the blood flowing, he picked up the child and rushed to Frances.

"We're going to have to take him to the doctor."

Once Frances had stopped the flow of blood with a towel, the three started to Dr. Morgan's office in Hokes Bluff. Both Jack and Frances had known Dr. Morgan for years. He had been the attending physician on several of the births Frances had overseen as a midwife.

"What are we going to tell the doctor about Daniel?" Jack asked as they rode in Frances' car to the doctor's office.

For Love of Daniel

"I'm going to tell him what we've been telling everyone else. Daniel is my nephew. I'll go in with Daniel. I'll talk to Dr. Morgan."

Once Frances signed in, Dr. Morgan, a late-fiftyish balding man wearing thick glasses, examined the child.

"A bad cut," he said. "He's going to need some stitches."

Moments later, he was sewing up the cut.

"Frances, I didn't know you had a child."

Frances froze at the question. She could feel her hands start to tremble.

"It's my younger sister's child," she said nervously. "I've been keeping him."

"You got a sister other than Mildred?" he asked. "I thought she was your only sister."

"Oh, no!" Frances lied, trying to stay calm. "I have a younger sister in Wetumpka."

"I never knew that," he said. "How long you had this boy?"

"A few years now," she replied.

Frances moved to change the subject.

"Dr. Morgan, do you think he could get an infection from this?"

"I'll give you some penicillin," Dr. Morgan replied. "That will take care of it."

Long silence.

"Your sister in Wetumpka," Dr. Morgan said. "What's her name?"

Frances could feel her throat tightening with the new question.

"Gladys," she lied again, wanting desperately to change the subject. "Is your son still down at the university?"

"Oh yes," he replied. "He's doing quite well in his studies. Made the dean's list again last semester. I'm expecting great things from him when he graduates."

Frances was relieved that he didn't return to the original subject.

"I'm sure he'll make a fine doctor," Frances said. "Just like this father."

Moments later, he was finished

"Okay," Dr. Morgan said. "Looks like he's all fixed again. Bring him back in two weeks and I'll remove the stitches."

Frances, relieved that the conversation was over, quickly left the office.

***

One day, when he was five, Daniel was sitting in Jack's lap when he noticed the eye patch for the first time. For a long moment, Daniel stared at the patch, then reached out and pulled it back so he could see inside Jack's deformed eye. Jack didn't move to stop him.

Daniel didn't react when he saw the deformed eye. For a long moment, he peered at it curiously. After a moment, he returned the patch to its original position, then he opened and closed the flap several times.

"I want to do it," Daniel said.

Jack removed the eye patch, shortened the string, and placed the patch over Daniel's eye. He ran to a mirror.

He laughed out loud when he saw himself.

For Love of Daniel

"I look like my daddy," he said with a squeal of joy.

Moments later, he returned the patch to Jack.

Once Jack had replaced the eye patch, Daniel hugged him.

"I love you, Daddy," he said.

School

In the early spring of 1961, it was time for Daniel to go to school. On the first day of enrollment, Frances took her pride and joy to Hokes Bluff Elementary School to enroll him in the first grade. At the school, she met the principal and, on the enrollment forms, she listed Jack as the child's father and herself as mother. Later, she met Daniel's first grade teacher and introduced Daniel. Frances explained she had done some home teaching and the child already knew his ABCs, how to count, and do simple math. The teacher said she felt the child would be a good student and she looked forward to having him in her class.

When Frances prepared to leave, the school principal explained that before the child was officially enrolled, he had to go to the county health department to get his vaccinations. Frances promised to take care of it. That afternoon, Frances and Daniel went into town and bought school books, new clothes, and school supplies to prepare him for his first year at school.

***

The following week, she took Daniel to the health department to get his vaccinations. After she filled out the forms, the clerk examined them.

For Love of Daniel

"The county health department doesn't have a birth certificate for your child. Can you provide one for our records?"

Suddenly, fear filled Frances' heart. This was the moment she had been dreading.

"I don't have one."

"Was the child born in Tallapoosa county?"

"No, he was born in Wetumpka County," Frances lied.

"We have to have a valid birth certificate before we can give a student a vaccination. It's a state law."

"Let me see what I can do."

When she returned home, the first thing she did was call Mildred.

"I was afraid of something like this," Mildred said. "Let's talk to the lawyer. We've got to know exactly where the law stands on this."

***

Attorney Cecil Grambling was a stocky, middle-aged man with a balding head, sagging jowls, and a constant scowl on his face. When Mildred, Jack, and Frances took a seat in his office two days later, he came straight to the point.

"How did y'all get possession of this child?"

Jack explained the episode with Suzanne.

"You haven't broken any laws," he said. "You can file a delayed birth certificate. It requires the date and place of birth, names of both parents, the child's name, and the signature of the person attending the birth."

John I. Jones

"That's all?" Mildred said. "We don't have to swear to anything?"

"No," the attorney continued. "Just fill out the form. Then you'll have to sign an affidavit stating that all of the information is true and correct. I wouldn't lie, although people do it all the time. Now, I should warn you that when the birth certificate reaches the state health department in Montgomery, they may have some questions."

"We can deal with that," Mildred said.

That afternoon, Mildred, Frances, and Jack went to the county health department and filed a delayed birth certificate. The mother was listed as Wanda Sue Smith and the father as "unknown." Afterward, both Jack and Frances signed the affidavit. Once they had an official birth certificate, Frances showed it to the clerk at the county health department and Daniel received his vaccinations.

***

Two weeks later, while Jack was at work, a sheriff's car appeared at Frances' house. A deputy got out and Frances met him at the door.

"I have a court summons," he said. "Sign here."

After signing, Frances opened the document and read it.

"You are being summoned to appear at the Tallapoosa Courthouse at 9 a.m. on October 3, 1961 for a custody hearing regarding the case of Daniel Jackson Griffin vs. The State of Alabama."

Moments later, Frances was calling Mildred.

For Love of Daniel

***

The following day, they were back in Cecil Grambling's office.

"The state wants to know why the child hasn't been in the orphanage in Montgomery for the past six years," the attorney said. "They're going to try to take the child."

"Why would the orphanage be so anxious to take custody?" Mildred asked.

"They want the $2,100 the state pays every year for the care of a new child. It all comes down to money. You're going to have to appear and answer charges as to why you have this child."

"Can they take Daniel away from Jack and Frances?" Mildred asked.

"They can if we don't put up a good case. In such cases, the first thing the court has to do is try to locate the child's mother. If they can locate her, they will determine whether she is fit to take custody. If they can't locate her, they'll have to find an alternative. Do you know anything about the mother's whereabouts?"

"No," France said. "Last time we saw her, she said she was going to California to be a movie star."

"California is a big state. Did she mention a city? Names of friends or relatives?"

"No," Frances replied. "She said to send a letter to Hollywood, California in her name and she would get it."

"We'll need to hire a private investigator to try to find her. That will take a while and it's expensive."

"How much is expensive?" Frances said.

"Around $250."

Frances inhaled.
"Whew!"
She looked to Jack.
"Can you help with that?"
"It will wipe out my savings, but I can do it."
"What about your fee?" Mildred asked.
"I'll need $500 to handle the case."
The two sisters looked at one another.
"We can handle that," Mildred said.

For Love of Daniel

Custody hearing

The Tallapoosa County Courthouse was a four-story, white-washed stucco building that took up an entire block on Broad Street between Eight and Ninth Avenues in Hamilton. When Circuit Judge Tom Murphy took his seat on the bench on the morning of Nov. 3, 1961, Jack, Frances, and Mildred were seated with their attorney at one of the counsel tables. On the opposite side of the aisle was Will Patterson, a tall, early-thirties man wearing glasses and smoking a pipe, representing the state. Once Judge Murphy rapped the gavel, the courtroom grew quiet.

"We're here today to decide the custody case of Daniel Jackson Griffin," the judge began. "Mr. Patterson, state your case."

"Your honor, first of all, I want to say I'm not sure what happened here. This child's birth record either fell through the cracks in the system or someone tried to deliberately hide it. Personally, I suspect the latter."

"What do you mean!" the judge asked.

"First, a birth certificate was not filed until six years after the birth. This child has been hidden from state purview for six years."

The judge shook his head.

"I can't see that any laws were broken. A delayed birth certificate has been filed. There is nothing unusual in that."

"This child should have been handed over to the state orphanage the day he was born."

"You're beating a dead horse," the judge said. "A birth certificate has been filed. What are your other objections?"

The attorney stopped, shuffled through some papers, then turned to face the judge again.

"Your honor, I have to tell the court that this child's care-givers, Jack Griffin and Frances Hathaway, not only have no legal right to this child, but they can't provide the same opportunities that are available at the state's orphanage."

"What are you saying?" the judge said.

"This couple is unfit to raise this child. This man lives alone in a rude shack outside of town. For transportation, he rides a bicycle. Furthermore, he works at a lowly job at a tire reclamation plant. The woman is fifty-seven years old, far too old to raise a young child. Also, she is a poor pensioner who ekes out a living from her small farm…"

The judge interrupted.

"That's not unusual. Most everybody I know around here just ekes out a living," he said with a grin. "Sometimes I think that's all I do… just eke out a living."

A ripple of laughter from the audience.

"Please continue," the judge said.

"This child should be in an environment where he can be around boys his own age. This child should be able to broaden his social horizons so he will have friends for the future. The services the orphanage offers are much broader and richer than what he currently has."

For Love of Daniel

He stopped and shuffled through some papers. For a long moment, he read a document, then turned back to the judge.

"Lastly, Jack Griffin and Frances Hathaway live in separate homes and are not married. That's not a proper environment for a small child."

"Hold it!" the judge said, turning to Jack and Frances' attorney.

"Mr. Grambling," he said. "Is that correct? Your clients aren't married?"

"That's correct, your honor."

For a moment, the judge peered at Jack and Frances, made a note on a legal pad, then returned to the state's attorney.

"Please continue."

"Finally, I want to impress upon the court that, as the state sees it, this child needs a structured, socially viable environment so he can grow up to be a stable, productive citizen. He doesn't have that at the moment. The orphanage will offer that."

Attorney Grambling rose to his feet.

"Your honor, for the past six years, Daniel Griffin has had a happy, healthy home environment with Jack Griffin and Frances Hathaway. He has developed a strong sense of self; he has a healthy social attitude and is an excellent student. While the circumstances through which this couple obtained the child are unusual, it does not diminish the fact that they have been loving, caring parents. I call Jack Griffin to the stand."

Moments later, Jack appeared in front of the bailiff and was sworn in.

"Name and occupation," Attorney Grambling said.

John I. Jones

"Jack Griffin. Loader operator at Cotton States Tires."

"Mr. Griffin, tell the court how you and your partner gained possession of this child."

Jack proceeded to tell the court how Suzanne had had the baby and left it with him and Frances. Once he was finished, the judge turned to him.

"Why didn't you reach out to the authorities once the baby was born?" the judge asked.

"Because Frances and I wanted a baby to care for. We had both been single all of our lives and wanted to have a family."

The judge continued.

"So when this wayward woman, this Wanda Sue Smith, drops an unwanted baby in your laps, you decided to keep it?"

"Yes, sir."

Satisfied, the judge turned back to Attorney Grambling.

"Proceed," he said.

"Now, Mr. Griffin. Tell the court about the life you and Miss Hathaway have had with this child over the past six years."

"Oh, we've been very happy. We do things together, he has chores to do on the farm, we go fishing a lot, and we build things. He has brought a lot of happiness into our lives."

"And the child refers to you and Frances as Daddy and Mother."

"Yes, sir."

"What about your finances? With your work at the reclamation plant and Frances' pension, do you have enough to make ends meet?"

For Love of Daniel

"Yes. And some left over."

Attorney Grambling turned, looked across the aisle.

"Your witness."

Attorney Patterson rose to address the court.

"Your honor, I'm saying to you, this case smells to high heaven. This couple, the circumstances under which they obtained the child as well as his current living environment are very unusual. I'm saying to you that you should rule that this child be sent to the state orphanage in Montgomery."

Judge Murphy looked askance at the attorney.

"Let me decide how to rule in this case," he said. "After all, I am the judge."

Attorney Patterson looked away.

Judge Murphy turned to the other attorney.

"Mr. Grambling, call your next witness."

Moments later, a tall, early thirties, dark-haired woman was sworn in.

"Name and occupation, please."

"Rebecca Medlin. Teacher at Hokes Bluff Elementary."

"You have been Daniel Griffin's first grade teacher for the past few months?"

"Yes."

"During that time, have you noticed any problems with this child? Emotional? Social problems? Any maladjustments?"

"No. Daniel is a very well-adjusted child. He plays and gets along well with the other children. He pays attention, minds the rules, and is an excellent student."

"He could read and write before he started school?" Attorney Grambling said.

"Yes."

"Did he tell you how he learned to read and write before going to school?"

"Yes. He said his mother taught him."

Attorney Grambling turned to the judge.

"Your honor, as you can see, Jack and Frances have tried to nurture this child in every way possible."

Then he returned to the witness.

"And when Daniel comes to school each day, his clothes are clean, he has all of the supplies he needs?"

"In every way."

"Does he ever say anything negative about his parents or give you any hint that he doesn't have a happy life at home?"

"No. None whatsoever."

"Thank you!" the attorney said. "You may be excused. I now call Frances Hathaway to the stand."

Moments later, Frances was sworn in.

"The state has said that your partner Jack Griffin only has a bicycle for transportation. Is that correct?"

"Yes."

"Is that a problem with caring for the child?"

"No."

"Please explain."

"I have a car. A good one. If one of us or Daniel needs anything, I always have transportation."

"And you can take Daniel wherever he needs to go."

"Yes."

Attorney Grambling looked across the aisle.

"Any questions?"

For Love of Daniel

"No."

"You may step down," the attorney said. "I now call Mildred Gibson to the stand."

Once she was sworn in, Mildred took a seat.

"Name and occupation."

"Mildred Gibson, director of Tallapoosa County Children's services."

"In your official capacity, have you had occasion to know Daniel Jackson Griffin?"

"Yes."

"Are you aware of any problems with this child? Emotionally? Socially? Health-wise?"

"No. In fact, Daniel is one of the most loving, well-behaved children I have ever seen."

"You are the sister of Frances Hathaway?"

"That's correct."

"Has your opinion of this child been colored by your relationship with Miss Hathaway?"

"No. Not in the least."

"You may be excused," the attorney said.

Mildred started to step down.

"Hold it!" the judge said. "I have some questions."

Mildred sat down again.

"You've been in charge of children's welfare services in Tallapoosa county for some twenty years now. In all that time, I have heard of very few cases where a birth went unreported. How did it happen that in this unreported case, the plaintiff happened to be your sister?"

"When I first became aware of the child, my sister said the child had been adopted."

"Did you ask her to show you the papers?"

"No. I felt she was telling the truth. She's my sister."

The judge peered at her for a long moment. He appeared satisfied.

"Okay," he said. Step down. Proceed, Mr. Grambling."

"We now call Hoyt Stephens to the stand."

An early forties, medium height man with a limp was sworn in.

"Name and occupation."

"Hoyt Stephens. Private investigator."

"Mr. Stephens, you have been searching for Wanda Sue Smith, the biological mother of this child, for over a month now?"

"That is correct."

"Where have you searched?"

"Los Angeles, the state of California, Nashville, Tennessee, and Birmingham. According to the information we have, those were the last places she was known to be."

"Did you locate her?"

"No."

"And you feel you have done an exhaustive search?"

"Yes. We have searched police, public, and utility records in each of those locations."

"You may be excused," Attorney Grambling said.

The private investigator stepped down.

"That's all, your honor," Grambling said. "In summation, I want to say it would be a terrible injustice to remove this child from the custody of Jack Griffin and Frances Hathaway. They love this child and have

For Love of Daniel

been caring surrogate parents to him for the past six years. As you can see from the testimony, he is a happy, healthy six-year-old. To deny this child his current environment would be unfair and unjust to both the child and his surrogate parents. That's all."

Judge Murphy turned to the other counsel.

"Mr. Patterson?"

The other attorney rose to address the court.

"Your honor," he began. "this child should never have been with these two people in the first place. Neither of them can offer this child a decent home. This child should be in the state orphanage in Montgomery, where he can be around boys his own age. What do these two have to offer?"

Attorney Grambling quickly rose to his feet.

"Their love, your honor. That's what they have to offer. The same love they have been offering this child for the past six years."

"Are you finished?" the judge asked.

"That's all," Attorney Grambling said.

The judge looked to the other attorney.

"Anything else, Mr. Patterson?"

"No, your honor."

Judge Murphy took a deep breath, then peered across the courtroom.

"In cases like this, the court would rather have one or both of the child's natural parents to take custody. Since the mother can't be located and the father is unknown, we've got to find alternatives. The state wants to place this child in the orphanage in Montgomery. While orphanages have certain advantages, I feel in this case it might be traumatic to suddenly move this child out of a loving home into a totally new environment.

From the testimony, it appears that the defendants have been good parents to this child and will continue to do so. The only question I have is this: why aren't these two married? Here they are raising a child together, but they are not bound by the bonds of holy matrimony?"

Attorney Grambling spoke up.

"My clients have been close friends for over ten years."

Judge Murphy continued.

"I'm aware of that, but it just doesn't look good to grant custody to two people who are not married. Marriage binds up a family into a total unit."

Attorney Grambling hesitated before he answered.

"Your honor, are you saying custody would be granted if my clients were married?"

"That's correct," the judge replied. "The child needs both a legal mother and a father."

"Your honor, would the court permit a short recess?"

"Granted!" the judge said, rapping his gavel. "Court is recessed for thirty minutes."

Five minutes later, Jack, Frances, Mildred, and their attorney were in a courthouse conference room.

"You heard the judge's words," Grambling said. "If you two will get married, he will grant custody."

Frances answered first.

"If that's what it takes to keep Daniel, I'll do it."

Jack inhaled. For a long moment, he looked away, then turned back to the attorney.

"Can Frances and I talk privately for a moment?"

"Sure."

For Love of Daniel

Jack and Frances moved out of earshot.

"There is something I wanted to tell you," he said in a low whisper.

"What's that?"

"I might not be able to do all the things you would expect out of a husband."

Frances looked at him.

"What do you mean? You have always done everything I asked of you."

"I mean… some things in the bedroom."

"There are no problems we can't solve if we work on them together."

Jack studied her for a moment.

"Do you really mean that?"

"Of course I mean it."

He didn't answer right away.

"This is our only chance," she said.

"Okay," he said finally. "If we can get Daniel and call him our child, I'll do it."

Twenty minutes later, all parties were back in court.

"Your honor, my clients have decided to be married," Attorney Grambling said.

"Good!" the judge replied. "That's a wise decision for the child's sake. Once you have provided me with a marriage certificate, I will grant custody to you."

***

The following morning, Jack, looking starkly out of character in a gray suit, and Frances, all six foot four of her decked out in a white velvet dress, were married in a simple ceremony at the Justice of the Peace's office in Hamilton. When the JP announced that the groom could kiss the bride, Jack stood on tiptoes and Frances leaned her towering frame way down to touch the lips of her new husband.

"Now you can start calling me Frances," she said.

Jack laughed.

"Yes, Frances. Whatever you say."

An hour later, an official copy of the marriage certificate was delivered to Judge Murphy. Two days later, Jack, Frances, and Mildred were back at the court clerk's office to sign the custody papers. Two weeks later, a county deputy appeared at Frances' house and delivered the official documents.

Over the next few weeks, Jack and Frances' lives underwent a set of wholesale changes. First, he gave up his house and moved all of his belongings into Frances' home. There wasn't room for all of his furniture, so they sold what they could, then stored the remainder in Frances' barn. Next came a period of adjustment as they worked out the details of bathroom time, getting Jack's personal belongings situated, and learning to live together. After several weeks of trial and error, they worked it out. It was for Daniel.

For Love of Daniel

Jack's Transformation

So Jack and Frances entered into a new phase in their lives with Daniel. In school, thanks to Frances' early tutoring, Daniel was an excellent student and, since he was a strong, sturdy child, he was very athletic. In the fall of 1962, after he enrolled in the second grade, Daniel announced that he wanted to sign up for the Pee-Wee football program. So, the following afternoon, when classes were dismissed, Frances met Daniel at school and, together, they met Coach Dan Watkins and his wife Elena.

"Now you know the mothers of players are expected to volunteer at the games," Elena said. "They sell drinks, hot dogs, programs, and such to fans. Will you be available to volunteer?"

"Oh yes," Frances replied. "I'll help any way I can."

"Also, you should become a member of the Parent-Teacher Association. The money for the boys' uniforms and equipment come out of the proceeds of PTA cake sales, raffles, and yard sales."

"I would like that."

So, just like that, Frances became a "football mom." Thereafter, on Friday afternoons, she was responsible for picking up Daniel at school after practice. Usually, she would arrive early and watch as Daniel and the other boys scrimmaged on the field. Once practice was over, she would talk to the coach.

"Daniel is a fine running back," Coach Watkins said one afternoon. "He's got speed, strength, and quick moves. He's going to be one of our best players."

Two days later, when Frances told Mildred about Daniel's new undertaking, she was quick to join in.

"I want to go to the games and see him play."

"We'll go together," Frances said.

***

Three weeks later, when the day of the first game of the season rolled around, Frances and Daniel couldn't wait.

"Daddy, my first game is Saturday. Are you going?"

"I don't think so."

"You've got to go, Daddy. I want you to see me play."

Jack looked at Frances.

Maybe later," Jack said.

"You've spent so much time playing football with me that you have to go see me in a real game."

Daniel turned to Frances.

"Mama! Can you get Daddy to go to my football game?"

"If he doesn't want to go, there is nothing I can do."

"Please!" the child begged.

"Maybe later," Jack said.

***

For Love of Daniel

Three hours later, when Daniel, Frances, and Mildred returned home from the game, Daniel bounded into the house. He was beside himself with excitement.

"Daddy!" he yelled "We won! We won!! I scored the winning touchdown."

"I'm so proud of you," Jack said.

"You've got to go to the next game and see me play. Will you go?"

"Maybe."

Daniel looked at Frances then dropped his head and went to his room.

"It would mean so much to Daniel if you would go to his games. He wants you to see him play."

"I really would like to..."

"What is it? What's stopping you?"

Jack peered at her for a long moment.

"You know the way kids are..."

"What do you mean?"

"Kids stare at my eye patch like I'm some kind of freak. They don't say anything, but I know what they're thinking."

Frances studied him for a moment.

"Jack! You're much more concerned about that eye patch than other people. People see it, but they accept it and go on. You're making far too much of it."

"I just don't feel comfortable."

"You've got to start going places with me and Daniel. We're a family now and we have to act like a family. You got dressed up for our wedding. I thought you looked very handsome."

Jack shook his head.

"I'm asking you to do this for Daniel."

"I know. That makes it even harder."

"At least give it a try."

Jack shook his head and looked away.

"Look! I'm going to make you a new eye patch. It will cover all of your eye socket."

"You don't have to do that."

"But I want to. It's for us. And Daniel."

Jack inhaled resignedly.

"And I want you to grow a mustache," she continued. "A thick, bushy one. With your dark hair, the mustache will make the eye patch less noticeable. Will you grow a mustache?"

"If it makes you happy…"

***

The following week, Frances went to a fabric shop in Hamilton and bought a small swath of heavy black cloth. After making a model, which covered Jack's entire eye, she sewed together several pieces then ironed and starched it to give it body. By then, Jack had the makings of a small mustache and it was time for him to try the new patch.

When he came in from work the following afternoon, Frances had the new patch ready. Jack took the new patch, examined it, then hung it over his eye and looked in the mirror. For a long moment, he didn't answer.

"What do you think?" Frances asked.

"You were right. The mustache makes the eye patch less noticeable."

For several moments, from various angles, he examined himself.

"It's better. Much better."

For Love of Daniel

Frances inspected the mustache.

"Let me trim your mustache a little. It needs to be more even at the ends."

Jack sat perfectly still while Frances did the trimming.

"Now. How's that?"

Jack returned to the mirror.

"Better. Much better."

"Now will you go to Daniel's next game with me and Mildred?"

"Yeah, I'll go."

***

At the game the following Saturday morning, Frances introduced Jack to the coach and then took her post at the refreshment stand. Once the game was underway, Jack and Mildred seated themselves in the stands. At first, Jack was quiet and standoffish, but once he saw Daniel and the team take the field, his interest quickened. Near the end of the first quarter, when Daniel took the ball on the nine-yard line and started around the left end for the goal line, Jack jumped to his feet, threw his fist in the air, and start cheering.

"Run, Daniel!" he yelled. "Run! Run!"

Seconds later, when Daniel crossed the goal line for a touchdown, Jack let out a loud whoop of pure joy and hugged Mildred.

"That's my boy!"

Once the game ended, the Hokes Bluff team had won again.

John I. Jones

On the way home, they stopped at a local burger joint. Jack and Frances waited in the car, while Daniel and Mildred went inside to place their orders.

"Now that wasn't so bad, was it?"

"No. I had fun. Nobody stared at my patch."

"Will you go to church with us on Sunday?"

"I'll give it a try."

***

The following Sunday would be a day Jack would always remember. Frances dressed him up in the gray suit he had worn at their wedding. She bought new shoes, underwear, and a blue tie. Once he was ready, she inspected him.

"You look very handsome, but you need some deodorant."

"Deodorant?"

"Yes. You can't go to church smelling like that."

Jack grimaced.

"I feel like a pig being led to slaughter."

"Now this is for me and Daniel."

Seconds later, Frances appeared with her deodorant and Jack used it.

When Jack arrived at church, he was reserved at first, but after he was welcomed by the minister and greeted warmly by several parishioners, he started to feel comfortable. That day, he sat in the pews alongside Daniel, Frances, and Mildred, and sang songs and listened to the sermon. He seemed right at home. When services were over, the minister was at the church steps to say good-bye.

"Jack, I hope you will come again."

For Love of Daniel

"I'll be back."

***

The following week, Frances, Daniel, and Jack went into town to pay bills. As they were walking up the street to the water department, Daniel stopped in front of a motorcycle shop.

"Daddy," he said. "Why don't you get a motorcycle? You wouldn't have to work as hard getting around."

"I don't think I could pass the vision test for a license."

"You could ask."

Later that afternoon, Jack called the Department of Motor Vehicles.

"A vision test is not required," the clerk said.

The following Saturday morning, Frances, Jack, and Daniel went into town and Jack bought a motorcycle. Once Jack paid for it, he fired it up, and he and Daniel rode it home. Daniel was ecstatic. Thereafter, he was always dreaming up reasons for him and Jack to take a ride. They would go to the store, run errands for Frances, and just go joy riding.

Only a week after Jack got the motorcycle, he stopped wearing overalls, denim shirts, and heavy work shoes. He began dressing in blue jeans with a silvery belt buckle and wearing motorcycle boots.

When Frances saw him for the first time, she asked what he was doing.

"I'm changing my look," he said.

Frances smiled happily and looked at Daniel. He returned the smile.

During football season, nothing made Daniel prouder than to arrive at practice on the motorcycle. When they would come roaring into the parking lot, the other boys would gather around to see the motorcycle.

"Rev 'er up, Jack!" the boys would urge. "Get 'er some gas!"

Jack would rev the engine into a mighty roar as the delighted youngsters would watch and applaud. Daniel was the envy of all the other boys.

***

During this period, Mildred continued to be an integral part of Daniel's life. Alongside Frances, she worked PTA events, was a regular at church with them on Sunday, and attended all of Daniel's football games. Jack and Mildred would sit together in the stands while Frances worked the refreshment counter.

At one game, Jack and Mildred rose to their feet when Daniel took the ball deep in Hokes Bluff territory and went racing down the sidelines.

"Run, Daniel!" Jack shouted. "Run!"

Mildred, caught up in the enthusiasm, joined in.

"Run, Andy!" she shouted. "Run!"

Jack looked at her.

"Andy?"

Mildred caught herself.

"I meant Daniel. They look so much alike."

***

Over the next four years, Jack and Frances' life began to blossom in ways they could never have

For Love of Daniel

imagined before they adopted Daniel. As a result of having the child, they suddenly became a part of the community and they found it extremely gratifying. For the first time, their lives were full. Frances was busy with her PTA duties; she was supervising cake sales, selling raffle tickets, cooking potluck meals for charity events, helping at yard sales, and attending meetings. During football season, she stayed busy with Daniel, volunteering her services at his games. Finally, church had become a "family activity" and every Sunday, she, Daniel, Jack, and Mildred were in attendance.

The biggest transformation was with Jack. During Daniel's second football season, Coach Watkins named Jack the "equipment coordinator." This meant, after each game, Jack was responsible for gathering helmets, shoulder pads, and other equipment, and seeing they were accounted for and safely stored for the next game. After his initial foray into church-going, he later became a parishioner and, when Daniel and Jack were baptized together, Jack became an official member.

During the 1965 football season, the Hokes Bluff team played in the state championship. For the event, Jack, Frances, Daniel, and Mildred went in her car to Birmingham and stayed overnight in a hotel. Frances and Mildred got a room together. Jack and Daniel got their own room. It was the first time Jack had ever stayed in a hotel.

In the game, the opposing team, the Butler Knights from Montgomery, were ahead at the half 14-7. At the end of the third quarter, Hokes Bluff recovered a fumble and scored a touchdown to even the score at 14-14. In the closing seconds, Hokes Bluff intercepted a

John I. Jones

pass and, after only two plays, Daniel ran a touchdown for the Hokes Bluff win.

The following morning, the victory photo appeared on the front page of the local newspaper. In the photo, along with the championship trophy, Coach Watkins, Daniel, and the other team members, there was Jack, eye patch perfectly in place, beaming at the camera.

Several days after the game, Mildred commented to Frances.

"I've never seen you so happy!!"

"My life is full," she said. "I've got a family. Someone to be with me and share my life. It has made me come alive."

"And I can't believe how much Jack has changed," Mildred continued. "He gets out, he goes places, he's not afraid to meet people anymore. He's a totally new person."

Frances peered at her.

"It's a miracle. An absolute miracle."

For Love of Daniel

Suzanne's Return

In late May of 1966, Daniel, at age 11, finished the sixth grade at Hokes Bluff Elementary. In the ceremony, the principal presented Daniel with a diploma and a small trophy for his performance on the Pee-Wee football team. Back at home, Frances threw a party. She baked a cake, prepared home-made ice cream, and hung festive garlands about the house. In attendance were some of Daniel's football friends, several classmates, and, of course, his Aunt Mildred. Once the party was over and the guests were gone, Frances was cleaning up the kitchen and Daniel was playing on the tire swing in the front yard, when a strange car appeared. It was a shiny black sedan with out-of-state plates and seemed starkly out of the place within the rough farm surroundings.

"Mama!" Daniel called. "Somebody is here."

Frances wiped her hands on her apron and went to the front door.

At the screen door, she stopped and peered outside. The driver's side door opened and a middle-aged man, dressed in a suit and looking very business-like, got out. Then he went to the passenger side and opened the door. Moments later, a smallish woman, late forties and looking very expensive, stepped out. Instantly, she surveyed the premises as if she had been there before. First, she looked across the road at Jack's old house, then she started across the yard to the door.

Frances, seeing the woman's approach, stepped out on the porch.

"Hello!" she said. "Can I help you?"

The woman didn't answer at first.

"Do you remember me?"

Frances peered closer.

"No."

"I'm Suzanne."

Now Frances recognized the woman.

"You're the woman that was here eleven years ago?"

"That's right."

"What do you want here?"

"I've come for my child."

"There is nothing here that belongs to you."

She looked at Daniel.

"That's my child. He belongs to me."

The man stepped forward.

"Miss Hathaway, my name is James Alverson. I'm Mrs. Rothstein's attorney. We have come here to get the child."

"I don't know what you're talking about," Frances said. "Y'all get out of my yard."

Suddenly, the screen door opened and Jack stepped out on the porch with a shotgun.

"Leave here!" Jack said. "Now!"

The two hesitated for a moment, then Jack stepped forward and pointed the shotgun.

"Get away from me and my family!" he shouted. "This is private property and you're trespassing."

"Mr. Griffin," the man said. "Please be reasonable."

For Love of Daniel

Jack, livid anger in his eyes, started down the steps. Once he was on the ground, he cocked the shotgun and pointed it.

"Wait! Wait!" Alverson said. "We don't want any trouble. We're leaving!"

Hurriedly, the attorney took Suzanne's arm and led her around the car to the passenger side. He opened the door.

"I'm going to get that child," Suzanne said. "He belongs to me."

"Get the hell out of here!" Jack said.

"You can either let me have him and I'll take him through the courts," Suzanne said.

"You're going to have to take him," Frances said.

"Go! Go!" Jack shouted.

Quickly, the two got into the car. The engine started. As it pulled away, the woman put her head out the window.

"I'll be back."

Daniel, Jack, and Frances watched as the car pulled away. Once the car was out of sight, Daniel turned to Frances.

"Mama! Who was that woman?"

"I don't know," she said.

"What did she mean when she said I belonged to her?"

"I don't know."

"Tell me," Daniel said. "I want to know."

"Some crazy woman. Don't worry about. Go ahead and play."

Frances looked to Jack for an answer.

"Go ahead and play, son," Jack said. "We'll talk about it later."

Daniel looked curiously from one to the other, then returned to his play.

***

That night, after Daniel was in bed, Jack and Frances sat on the front porch in the darkness. As always, the frogs were singing to the night.

"The cat's out of the bag," Frances said. "What are we going to tell Daniel?"

"If she takes us to court, we're going to have to tell him the truth. Let's see how far she goes."

***

The following Monday afternoon, while Jack and Frances were in the garden picking pole beans, a county sheriff's car pulled into the yard. Sheriff Sam Gilbreath got out. They went to meet him.

"Morning, sheriff," Jack said.

"Morning, Jack. I got some court papers to serve you."

"What's it all about?"

"Looks like a woman is suing you for custody of that child."

He handed the summons to Jack.

"Sign here!" the sheriff said.

Jack signed and the sheriff drove away.

They examined the document.

"Let's talk to Mildred," Frances said.

For Love of Daniel

***

The following morning, Jack, Frances, and Mildred were back in Cecil Grambling's office.

"As the child's biological mother, I have to tell you she can probably get custody."

"She's not going to take that child," Mildred said. "He means too much to us."

"We've got our work cut out for us," the attorney said. "It's going to be a tough fight."

That night, they discussed it with Daniel.

"Is this woman going to take me away from you and Daddy?"

"No!" Mildred said. "Not if we can help it. We love you with all of our hearts and we're not going to lose you."

"How can she take me away? Y'all are my mother and father and my aunt."

"There is something we have to tell you," Frances said.

Over the next twenty minutes, they explained to Daniel the circumstances of his birth. Once they had finished, the child studied them for a long moment.

"So y'all are not really my mother and father?"

"That's right," Jack said.

"But I don't want to live with somebody else. Somebody I don't know. Somebody I've never learned to love. I'm happy with y'all. I love y'all."

"And we love you and want to keep you," Jack said. "But there is a chance we may not be able to. We'll have to see what happens in court."

Suddenly, Daniel burst into tears. Then he quickly got up, went to his room, and slammed the door.

The Hearing

Three weeks later, on June 22, 1966, Circuit Judge Tom Murphy called the custody hearing to order in the same courtroom where the first case had been heard five years earlier. At one counsel table sat Jack, Frances, Mildred, and their attorney. Across the aisle sat Suzanne, decked out in an expensive designer dress and shoes, and her attorney. The first witness was Frances.

"Isn't it true," Attorney Grambling said, "that eleven years ago, Mrs. Rothstein left the child with you and your husband with the agreement the child was yours to keep?"

"Yes, sir."

"And, at the time, she appeared to have no love for the child. No affection? No sense of caring? No maternal attitude? She just wanted to be free of the baby?"

"Yes."

"Please tell the court her exact words."

"She said she was going to Hollywood to become a movie star and she didn't have time to take care of a child."

"Didn't have time for a child…" Attorney Grambling said, repeating and turning to the judge. "Now I ask you, your honor… does that sound like the kind of woman who is fit to raise a child?"

Attorney Alverson rose to his feet.

For Love of Daniel

"Objection, your honor," he said. "That happened eleven years ago. My client is not the same person today she was eleven years ago. She is an older, wiser woman now."

"Sustained."

Grambling took a deep breath then turned back to Frances.

"During the last eleven years, you and your husband have loved and cared for this child. You have given him food, clothing, and shelter, attended to his personal needs, and sent him to school. Is that correct?"

"Yes, sir."

Grambling turned to the other attorney.

"Your witness."

"No questions," Alverson said. "I now call Mrs. Suzanne Rothstein."

Seconds later, Suzanne was sworn in.

"Name and occupation?"

"Suzanne Rothstein, Hollywood film producer."

"Mrs. Rothstein," Attorney Alverson said. "Please explain to the court why you feel you now have a right to legal custody of this child."

For a moment, Suzanne looked around the courtroom, then began speaking.

"I made a mistake eleven years ago, your honor. A terrible mistake. At the time I left my child, I was just a young, naïve woman who didn't know what I wanted in this world. I had my head set on dreams of Hollywood stardom. I had stars in my eyes and I couldn't see anything else."

Grambling interrupted.

"Your honor, Mrs. Rothstein was thirty-seven years old when she abandoned this child. That's not what I would consider young and naïve."

"Objection, your honor," Alverson shot back. "Counsel is not a witness here."

"Sustained."

Alverson continued.

"Now, Mrs. Rothstein, please tell the court how your situation has changed."

"Now I'm married to a successful Hollywood producer. We have a beautiful house in Beverly Hills, we go to parties at the homes of famous actors and directors, and we have vacation homes in Hawaii and Florida."

The judge studied her.

"In short, you're quite a bit wealthier now than you were when you abandoned the child."

"Yes," Suzanne said.

Attorney Grambling rose to his feet.

"Your honor," he said. "Mrs. Rothstein can offer this child things that money can buy, but she can't offer him the love of a caring mother and father."

"How would you know what she can offer?" Alverson shot back.

"Because I've personally watched my clients care for this child for the past six years. They have been good, loving parents."

"Objection, your honor," Alverson said. "Please remind counsel that he is not a witness in this case."

"Sustained!" the judge said. "Mrs. Rothstein, let me ask you a question. During all those years you were building a career in Hollywood, did you have any concern for the welfare of the child? Didn't you wonder about him? If he was being fed and sheltered? If he was even alive?"

"Yes," she said. "Many, many nights I have lain awake wondering about Daniel. All the time, I was hoping and praying he was healthy and happy."

Grambling was quick to respond.

"Your honor, she says she spent many wakeful nights wondering about the welfare of this child. During all those nights she was worrying, she never bothered to call and check on the child. She never bothered to write a letter or send money for the child's welfare."

Alverson rose to respond.

"Your honor, Mrs. Rothstein is a senior vice president at Monogram Studios in Hollywood. She is a very busy woman."

"If she was as concerned as she claims," Grambling continued. "She could have communicated with the child. At least a phone call. A letter."

"Your honor, as I explained, Mrs. Rothstein is a very busy woman."

Judge Murphy returned to the witness.

"So what makes you think you can be a good mother to this child at this late stage?"

"First of all, I'm the child's natural mother. He is my flesh and blood and I love him. Next, as an older, wiser person, I'm at the age I can be a good mother. Most of all, I want to be a good mother and share my life with him."

"How can you say you love this child when you haven't seen him for the past eleven years?" the judge asked.

Suzanne was quick to respond.

"Because I'm his natural mother. I want him to know me as his natural mother. That's the only reason I need."

Judge Murphy turned to Attorney Grambling.

"Do your clients question the fact that this woman is, in fact, the biological mother of the child?"

"No, your honor," Grambling replied. "My clients readily admit that this was the woman who had the child, then abandoned it to my clients' care eleven years ago."

"All right," Judge Murphy said.

"Your witness," Grambling said.

"No questions."

"Summations?" the judge said.

Attorney Grambling stepped in front of the bench.

"Your honor, I want to say to the court that it would be a gross injustice to remove this child from the care of my clients. Over the past eleven years, this child has grown to love them as if they were his natural father and mother. To put the child into the care of a new caregiver who the child has never known and never loved would be highly unfair to both the child and my clients."

"Mr. Alverson?"

Mrs. Rothstein's attorney stepped in front of the bench.

"Your honor, there is no question that my client is the natural mother of this child. All parties agree to that. I must impress upon you that the laws of the state of Alabama make it very clear that if a natural parent is available and of sound mind, the custody of a child should go to that parent. The law cannot be circumvented."

For Love of Daniel

"I know what the law says," Judge Murphy replied. "Is that all?"

"That's all, your honor," Attorney Alverson replied.

"Very well," the judge said.

The judge's eyes swept across the courtroom. He looked at the clock.

"I'm going to adjourn for lunch. At 1 p.m., I will return with my ruling. Court dismissed until then."

Ten minutes later, spectators and courtroom combatants had spilled out into the courthouse corridor. Jack, Frances, and Mildred were talking among themselves when Suzanne and her attorney stepped out. The moment Frances saw Suzanne, she went directly to her.

"You low-life slut!! Do you have any idea what you're going to do to this child?"

Suzanne quickly turned to face her.

"What does it matter to you?" she said. "That child belongs to me. I'm his real mother. Not you."

"I've watched this child grow up for the past eleven years," Frances said. "I know this child has been happy and healthy all that time."

"You don't know crap!" Suzanne said with a laugh. "You're just one more redneck stuck back in these God-forsaken hills. I'm going to get Daniel and you can't stop me. I don't want my son growing up eating beans and cornbread for the rest of his life."

Instantly, Mildred, who had been listening, stepped up.

"You're not getting that child!"

Suzanne was quick to respond.

John I. Jones

"Who's going to stop me? Some dime store social worker like you? I wipe my feet on people like you every day. You're just as big a redneck as these two... The amazon and Mr. One-eye."

Suzanne turned to go. Mildred stepped forward, grabbed Suzanne's arm, and pulled her face close to her own.

"You heard what I said."

"Get your God-damn hands off me!" Suzanne screamed, angrily slapping Mildred's hand away. "Who do you think you're talking to? I buy and sell rednecks like you every day."

Quickly, Suzanne turned, and she and her attorney started down the corridor.

"You're not taking that child!" Mildred said.

Instantly, fire in her eyes, Suzanne turned on her.

"You freaking redneck! I'll kick your butt nine ways from Sunday!"

Suddenly, she rushed forward and swung her hand at Mildred's face. Instantly, Mildred backed away.

Suzanne's attorney rushed forward.

"No! No! Mrs. Rothstein!" he said, grasping Suzanne's arm to keep her away from Mildred. "This woman is a member of law enforcement."

"I don't care who she is," Suzanne said. "No redneck tells me what to do."

"Come on!" the attorney said.

For a moment, Suzanne peered angrily at Mildred, then, as her attorney pulled her arm, she reluctantly turned and started down the corridor.

"I'll see you in hell before I let you take that child," Frances shouted.

Suzanne didn't look back.

For Love of Daniel

"That bitch!! That low-life slut!!" Mildred said under her breath as she watched Suzanne disappear down the courthouse corridor.

***

Promptly at 1 p.m., Judge Murphy returned to the bench and the courtroom combatants returned to their places at the counsel tables.

"I remember this case from six years ago," he began. "At the time I made my ruling, I explained that I was granting custody to Jack and Frances Griffin only because the child's natural mother couldn't be found. Now that has changed.

"I commend the defendants for their efforts to care for this child over the past eleven years. If there were more people who would undertake the care of abandoned children like these two, there wouldn't be nearly as many lonely children in orphanages and state welfare programs.

"On the other hand, the law is the law and I must abide by it. The law states that, in such cases, if either of the biological parents are available to care for the child, custody must be granted to that parent. I know this may seem harsh and unfair to the defendants and the child, but the law is the law. With that in mind, I hereby grant custody of the child, Daniel Jackson Griffin, to Mrs. Suzanne Rothstein."

A hush fell across the courtroom.

At the words, Frances collapsed in sobs. Quickly, Mildred and Jack moved to console her. A big smile broke across Suzanne's face and she hugged her attorney.

Judge Murphy continued:

"Mr. Grambling, when and where can your clients turn over the child to Mrs. Rothstein?"

"Some time will be necessary to gather the child's belongings and get him ready," the attorney said.

"How much time?"

The attorney turned to Frances.

"How much time will you need to get the child ready?"

"Two days," she replied. "Can they come to my house to get him?"

The attorney turned back to the judge.

"Two days, your honor," the attorney replied. "Can Mrs. Rothstein come to the Griffin home to take custody?"

"Actually, we prefer a neutral location," Attorney Alverson replied.

Quickly, Suzanne tapped her attorney's shoulder and whispered in his ear.

The attorney turned back to the judge.

"That's fine, your honor," he said. "My client is agreeable that the hand-over of the child can take place at the Griffin home."

"Very well," Judge Murphy said. "Hand-over of the child will take place on June 24 at 10 a.m. at the Griffin home on Highway 17. That's two days away."

***

That afternoon, when Daniel came in from school, Jack, Frances, and Mildred sat down with him in the living room.

"We have bad news," Mildred began.

For Love of Daniel

"What is it?"

"We were at court today and the judge said you're going to have to go with that woman."

Daniel looked from one to the other.

"They're going to take me away from y'all?"

Frances nodded

"It's a court order," Mildred said. "There's nothing we can do."

The words had not fully registered with the child.

"Why am I going away? I don't even know this woman."

"We know that," Frances said. "But there is nothing we can do."

Suddenly, Daniel burst into tears and ran into Frances' arms.

"Please, Mama," he pleaded, grasping her tightly. "Don't let them do this to me!"

"I'm sorry," Frances said. "We love you and want you to stay with us, but there's nothing we can do. We've got to follow the law. The day after tomorrow, she will come here to get you. You'll have to be ready."

"Where is she taking me?"

"I don't know," Frances said. "Now I want you to straighten up and be brave about this. We've got to follow the law."

"Oh, Mama," he said, burying his face in Frances' bosom. "I love you so much."

***

The following night, the night before the handover, Jack, Frances, and Mildred were sitting on the front porch at Frances' house. They talked in the darkness while a chorus of frogs croaked loudly down at the river. They were having a conversation they could never have imagined a year earlier.

"It's going to kill me to see her take Daniel," Frances said.

"Me too," Jack said. "When Daniel goes away, our lives will go away."

"We've got to stop her," Mildred said. "One of us is going to have to kill her."

For several moments, they sat quietly in the darkness. The only sound was the bullfrogs.

"Let me kill her," Jack said finally. "Tomorrow I'll hide behind the woodpile and, when she and her lawyer pull up in their big car, I'll drop her. I've got punkin' balls for my shotgun. She will die instantly. With her out of the way, Daniel will be able to stay with y'all. Y'all can take care of him until he's grown."

Mildred looked at him.

"Then you'll spend the rest of your life in prison and Daniel won't have a father. That child is going to need a mother and a father over the next ten years."

They were quiet again. Down at the river, the frogs continued their chorus.

"Maybe I could hit her with my car," Frances said. "I could make it look like an accident."

"There's no time for that," Mildred said. "Things like that take time to plan and pull off. They'll be here in the morning."

They were quiet again. The only sound was the croaking frogs.

For Love of Daniel

"Then it would be you that goes to prison rather than Jack. Then Daniel wouldn't have a mother. Remember, we're doing this for Daniel."

They were quiet again.

"So what do we do?" Frances said.

"I don't know," Mildred said. "We have to follow the law."

Frances peered at her.

"You always say that, but this time, the law has let us down. So I ask you again, what do we do?"

They were quiet again. The frogs grew louder.

"I'll do it," Mildred said finally. "I'll take care of it."

"What are you going to do?" Frances said.

"I don't know, but I'll see that it's taken care of."

They were quiet again. The bullfrogs were croaking away.

Suddenly, Mildred burst into tears. Jack and Frances peered at one another. In the darkness, they could see Mildred wiping her eyes.

"What's wrong?" Frances asked.

"There's something I have to tell y'all," Mildred said. "When I was at the doctor's last week, he said I have a cancer in my stomach. He said it was inoperable and I didn't have long to live."

"Oh, no!" Frances said. "How long?"

"Six, maybe seven months."

"Oh, God! What did I do to deserve all of this grief?"

"We've all got our crosses to bear in this world. I've borne mine long enough."

"What are you going to do about Suzanne?" Jack asked.

"I'm going to see that she is put away. I'm going to see that she is put away for good."

Down by the river, the bullfrogs were suddenly silent.

For Love of Daniel

The Hand-over

The following morning, promptly at 10 a.m., two county sheriff's cars and the big black sedan pulled up in the front yard at Frances' house. Suzanne, in a white cashmere dress, and her attorney got out and waited at the sedan. Moments later, Sheriff Gilbreath was walking across the yard to the front door steps. The front door was open.

He called.

"Jack? Frances?"

Jack appeared at the door.

"Is the child ready?"

"He's ready," Jack said. "We're coming right out."

Moments later, Frances, Mildred, and Daniel stepped out on the front porch. Daniel, looking very teary-eyed, was neatly dressed and had a suitcase. Jack, Frances, Mildred, and Daniel strode down the steps to meet the waiting sheriff.

Once they were on the ground, Frances handed the suitcase to the sheriff, then she turned back to Daniel for a final good-bye.

"Oh, Mama," Daniel said, crying softly. "I love you."

"I love you too," Frances said, kissing him on the forehead. "Now be brave. Take the sheriff's hand and go with him."

Daniel turned and took the sheriff's hand. Then together, they began walking toward Suzanne, who was waiting at the black sedan. Once they reached her, the sheriff gave her Daniel's hand. In the other hand, she took the suitcase. For a moment, she peered down at the child, then seeing his tears, she took a handkerchief from her purse and knelt in front of him.

"Let me dry your tears. I'm your mother now. Everything is going to be just fine."

Daniel, his eyes red from crying, looked hatefully at Mrs. Rothstein, then waited as she wiped away his tears. Once finished, she took his hand again and, together, they started walking toward the black sedan. After several steps, Daniel suddenly turned and looked back at Frances. Upon seeing her, he jerked his hand free of Mrs. Rothstein's and started running back across the yard to Frances.

"Mama! Mama!" he screamed.

Suzanne turned.

"Come back here! You belong to me now!"

Instantly, Suzanne started running across the yard in pursuit of the child. At the very instant Daniel reached Frances and ran into her arms, Mrs. Rothstein was only a few steps behind him.

Suddenly, a pistol shot rang out.

Blam!!

At the sound of the shot, the front of Mrs. Rothstein's white cashmere dress turned a crimson red as her life's blood flooded into the innermost threads of the fabric. For an instant, her face took on a look of shocked surprise, then her eyes rolled back into her head and she fell face first at the feet of Frances, Daniel, Jack, and Mildred. Instantly, a pool of warm blood began to form under her prostrate form and seep into the dirt and gravels of the driveway.

"Mildred!" Sheriff Gilbreath shouted, moving toward her. "Drop that gun!"

The .45 revolver Mildred was holding fell to the ground.

The sheriff stepped forward and picked it up.

"What are you doing taking the law into your own hands?" he said. "You're supposed to let the law dispense justice."

Mildred peered at him.

"Sometimes the law doesn't dispense justice."

The sheriff drew a deep breath.

"Yeah. Maybe you're right."

Then he motioned to a deputy to take her into custody.

"You're under arrest for murder," the deputy said.

Once the deputy placed handcuffs on Mildred's wrists, he turned back to the sheriff.

"What about her?" he said, indicating Suzanne. "Want me to call an ambulance?"

"Ambulance won't do her any good. Call the coroner."

For a moment, Sheriff Gilbreath turned and took a step to get a closer view of Suzanne's body.

"Right through the heart. Those .45 slugs really make a mess."

Satisfied, he turned to address Frances.

"Frances, you and Jack go ahead and keep that boy until I can talk to the judge. I should know something official by tomorrow."

John I. Jones

***

Two days later, Judge Murphy granted permanent custody to Jack and Frances. In the ruling, he said, now that the child's birth mother was deceased, it was only right that Daniel should continue to live with his long-term caregivers. So, over the next ten years, Jack and Frances finished raising Daniel and, over those years, he made them very proud. At Hokes Bluff High, he was an excellent student and football star and, upon graduation, won a football scholarship to the University of Alabama, where he studied law. After graduation, he married his high school sweetheart and set up a practice near Gadsden. Years later, he would be elected a state senator and finally a circuit judge. Over those same years, Jack and Frances lived happily to be a ripe old age.

***

Mildred didn't live long enough to stand trial. At her arraignment, the judge set the trial date for Jan 3, 1967. After spending less than a week in the county jail, her condition worsened and she was transferred to a hospital in Birmingham, where she was due to begin radiation treatments. The night before the treatments were set to begin, Daniel, Frances, and Jack visited her.

"This is probably good-bye," Mildred said. "I'm not sure how many of these treatments my body can take, but it's my only choice. I love y'all. Over these past few years, y'all are the only family I've had."

After several days of radiation treatments, Mildred appeared to show some improvement, but, only

For Love of Daniel

days after the seeming improvements, she slipped into a coma and died peacefully in her sleep on December 28, 1966. She was buried at the Old Harmony Baptist Church, the country church on Highway 17 where they had worshipped together.

The following spring, Jack and Frances had a headstone erected at her grave. Frances said she had requested something simple and memorable. Once erected, the headstone read:

Mildred Dianne Gibson

1899-1966

Thanks for Daniel!!

The End

Dear Reader:

Thanks for taking the time to read my novella *For Love of Daniel*.

If you enjoyed it, please consider telling your friends or posting a short review.

Reviews make a difference.

It only takes a few words and it can help enormously.

Without your reviews and favorable mentions, my hard work might go unnoticed.

Thanks a million for your support.

John I. Jones

For Love of Daniel

A * JIJ * Book
Copyright 2018 by John Isaac Jones
All rights reserved. No part of this book may be reproduced or transmitted in any form by any means, electronic or mechanical, including photocopying and recording, or by any information storing and retrieval system, except as may be expressly permitted by the 1976 Copyright Act or by the publisher. Requests for permission should be sent to johni@johnisaacjones.com

Photo attribution: Family silhouette © Can Stock Photo / Paha_L

This book is a work of fiction and any resemblance to persons, living or dead, or places, events, and locales is purely coincidental. The characters are reproductions of the author's imagination and used fictitiously.
Manufactured in the United States of America
First edition/First printing

www.ingramcontent.com/pod-product-compliance
Lightning Source LLC
Chambersburg PA
CBHW020659300426
44112CB00007B/448